ERNEST CHARLES SHEARMAN
(1859-1939)
AN ANGLO-CATHOLIC ARCHITECT

AN ILLUSTRATED INTRODUCTION
TO HIS LIFE AND WORK

BY

JOHN SALMON

NUMBER 6 IN A SERIES OF OCCASIONAL PAPERS

FIRST PUBLISHED IN 2009
BY THE ANGLO-CATHOLIC HISTORY SOCIETY
Revd Dr. Perry Butler, Chairman
Brent Skelly, Secretary and Treasurer,
24, Cloudesley Square, London N1 OHN
email: skelly785@btinternet.com.
Edited by Michael Yelton

British Library Cataloguing in Publication data

A catalogue record for this book is available
from the British Library

ISBN: 978-0-9560565-0-4
Pre print by Trevor Preece: Trevor@epic-gb.com
Printed and bound by 4edge Ltd, Hockley. www.4edge.co.uk

DEDICATION

To the memory of Father G. Napier Whittingham, the first Parish Priest of St. Silas the Martyr, Kentish Town, London (1907-1930) who had the insight to engage E.C. Shearman as architect; and to Father Graeme C. Rowlands, whose ministry there since 1989 has restored this church into a shrine of devotion and worship.

Portrait Ernest Charles Shearman

PREFACE AND ACKNOWLEDGEMENTS

This task started as a personal exploration following my introduction to the church of St. Silas the Martyr, Kentish Town, London, during 1992. In 1995 I was asked by Father Graeme Rowlands to undertake the work of producing a guide-book for the church and in preparation for this I decided I needed to review all the available parish papers. E.C. Shearman featured quite frequently in these papers and this whetted my appetite for more information about him. My curiosity was further aroused by the lack of information available on Shearman elsewhere. The editors of *Pevsner* gave scant reference to the six London churches which were accredited to him. Other books made similar brief reference to the architect. My first building block was his obituary in *Architect and Building News* dated 28th April 1939, which was equally brief. I decided that Shearman had been neglected and ignored and that his work needed to be more widely known.

I wish to acknowledge the help given to me by the parish priests of the Shearman churches, who have provided details of their records and allowed me the opportunity to photograph whenever necessary. I offer particular thanks to Father E. James Alcock of St. Gabriel, Acton, who has always been most keen that I should continue this work; to Father Gerald Reddington and Richard Bowden at St. Barnabas, North Ealing; to Robert Black at St. Francis of Assisi, Isleworth, and to the Revd. Jeremy Howat (former priest at Holy trinity, Lomas de Zamora, Buenos Aires) for taking photographs and providing information about the church. I am also grateful to those who have written church guidebooks or otherwise provided information about them, particularly Marjorie H. Cole for The story of a church, St. Matthew's Wimbledon and Mr. David G. Robbins for further information on the church; Richard Bowden for A Guide to St. Barnabas Parish Church [North Acton]; Edward Harcourt Bustard for St Barnabas Church, Temple Fortune; and the Department of National Heritage for their report on St. Francis dated 14th January 1994.

Above all, I sincerely thank Shearman's granddaughter Jeane Duffey, who has been an invaluable source of information.

Shearman's churches are still living places of worship and as such they have moved forward with time. As well as describing their architectural features, I have recorded information about other items of interest which are not by Shearman. I hope that by their inclusion further appeal will be generated in readers who visit these churches. I have not answered all the questions about Shearman – no doubt I have only touched the surface. There are a number of intriguing mysteries about him and possibly by bringing this man out of the shade, further information will become available which can expand our knowledge of this once ignored and neglected architect.

John Salmon

Shearman Family Tree

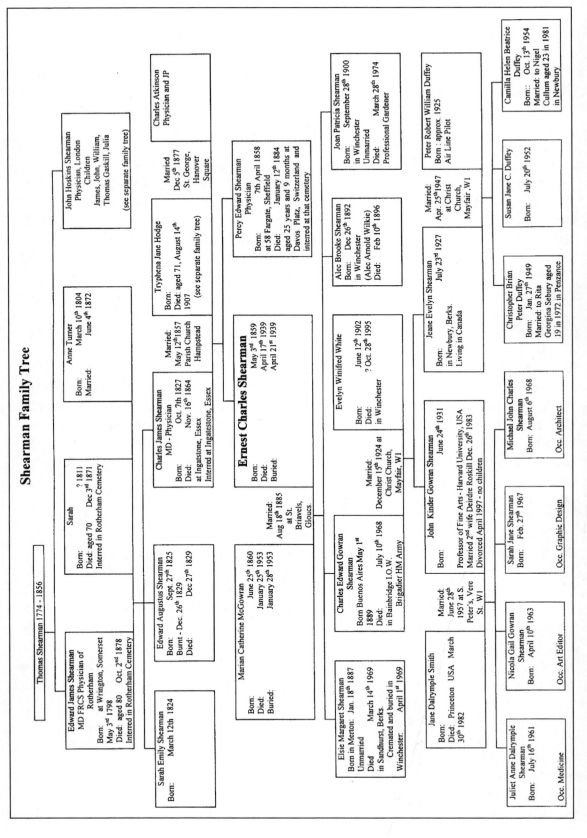

Thomas Shearman 1774 - 1856

Edward James Shearman
MD FRCS Physician of Rotherham
Born: at Wrington, Somerset May 3rd 1798
Died: aged 80 Oct. 2nd 1878
Interred in Rotherham Cemetery

Sarah
Born:
Died: aged 70 Dec 3rd 1871
Interred in Rotherham Cemetery

?1811

Anne Turner
Born: March 10th 1804
Married:
June 4th 1872

John Hoskins Shearman
Physician, London
Children
James, John, William, Thomas Gaskill, Julia
(see separate family tree)

Charles Atkinson
Physician and JP

Sarah Emily Shearman
Born: March 12th 1824

Edward Augustus Shearman
Born: Sept. 27th 1825
Burnt - Dec. 26th 1829
Died: Dec 27th 1829

Charles James Shearman
MD - Physician
Born: Oct. 7th 1827
Died: Nov. 16th 1864
at Ingatestone, Essex
Interred at Ingatestone, Essex

Married:
May 12th 1857
Parish Church
Hampstead

Tryphena Jane Hodge
Born:
Died: aged 71, August 14th 1907
(see separate family tree)

Married
Dec 5th 1877
St. George, Hanover Square

Percy Edward Shearman
Physician
Born: 7th April 1858 at 58 Fargate, Sheffield
Died: January 12th 1884 aged 25 years and 9 months at Davos Platz, Switzerland and interred at that cemetery

Marian Catherine McGowran
Born: June 25th 1860
Died: January 25th 1953
Buried: January 28th 1953

Married:
Aug 18th 1885
at St. Briavels, Gloucs.

Ernest Charles Shearman
Born: May 3rd 1859
Died: April 17th 1939
Buried: April 21st 1939

Evelyn Winifred White
Born: June 12th 1902
Died: ? Oct. 28th 1995
in Winchester

Alec Brooke Shearman
Born: Dec 26th 1892 in Winchester
(Alec Arnold Wilkie)
Died: Feb 10th 1896

Joan Patricia Shearman
Born: September 28th 1900 in Winchester
Unmarried
Died: March 28th 1974
Professional Gardener

Elsie Margaret Shearman
Born in Merton: Jan. 18th 1887
Unmarried
Died March 14th 1969
in Sandhurst, Berks.
Cremated and buried in Winchester. April 1st 1969

Charles Edward Gowran Shearman
Born Buenos Aires May 1st 1889
Died: July 10th 1968 in Bainbridge I.O.W.
Brigadier HM Army

John Kinder Gowran Shearman
Born: June 24th 1931 in Newbury, Berks.
Professor of Fine Arts - Harvard University, USA
Married 2nd wife Deirdre Roskill Dec. 26th 1983
Divorced April 1997 - no children

Married:
December 15th 1924 at Christ Church, Mayfair, W1

Jeane Evelyn Shearman
Born: July 23rd 1927 in Newbury, Berks.
Living in Canada

Married:
Apr. 25th 1947 at Christ Church, Mayfair, W1

Peter Robert William Duffey
Born: approx. 1925
Air Line Pilot

Camilla Helen Beatrice Duffey
Born: Oct. 13th 1954
Married: to Nigel Cullum aged 23 in 1981 in Newbury

Susan Jane C. Duffey
Born: July 20th 1952

Christopher Brian Peter Duffey
Born: Jan. 27th 1949
Married: to Rita Georgina Sebury aged 19 in 1972 in Penzance

Michael John Charles Shearman
Born: August 6th 1968
Occ: Architect

Sarah Jane Shearman
Born: Feb. 27th 1967
Occ: Graphic Design

Jane Dalrymple Smith
Born: Princeton USA March
Died: Princeton USA March 30th 1982

Married:
June 28th 1957 at S. Peter's, Vere St. W1

Nicola Gail Gowran Shearman
Born: April 10th 1963
Occ: Art Editor

Juliet Anne Dalrymple Shearman
Born: July 16th 1961
Occ: Medicine

ERNEST CHARLES SHEARMAN
A BIOGRAPHY

The first document which I discovered in relation to Ernest Charles Shearman was his obituary in *Architect and Building News* for 28th April 1939, which gives the basic facts about him:

"It is with regret that we have to announce the death of Mr. Ernest Charles Shearman, A.R.I.B.A. Born in 1859, Shearman was articled to Charles Barry, F.S.A., and was his assistant for nine years. From 1888 to 1891 he was architect to the Buenos Aires Great Southern Railway; besides railway works he was responsible in the Argentine for a number of ecclesiastical and domestic buildings. He was elected Associate of the R.I.B.A. in 1892. Mr. Shearman was the architect of St. Matthew's Church Wimbledon; St. Silas the Martyr Church, Camden Town; the Lady Chapel of St. Jude's Church, Birmingham; Brandon Rectory, Suffolk; Manea Vicarage, Cambridge; the Home for Epileptics at Chalfont St. Peter; and houses at Winchester, Newmarket, Birmingham, Harrow, and Bexhill".

Ernest Charles Shearman was born on 3rd May 1859, the son of Charles James Shearman and Tryphena Jane, née Hodge. The date of his death was 17th April 1939, shortly before what would have been his eightieth birthday.

Information, although scanty, has allowed a family tree to be compiled back to Shearman's great-grandfather, who was a Thomas Shearman (1774–1856). The only information available about Thomas Shearman is that he had two sons, Edward James Shearman and John Hoskins Shearman. It is not known which son was born first, but Edward James (Shearman's grandfather) was born at Wrington, Somerset on 3rd May 1798 and died aged 80 on 2nd October 1878.

Both these brothers were Physicians, Edward James in Rotherham and John Hoskins in London. It is possible that their father was also a Physician. It will be seen that the medical profession runs through the Shearman family.

Shearman's grandfather is known to have had three children by his first wife Sarah. The children were Sarah Emily, born 12th March 1824, Edward Augustus, born 27th September 1825 and Charles James, born 7th October 1827, who was to become Ernest Charles Shearman's father. It would appear that during 1909 Shearman had become interested in his own ancestry and had written to his cousin Julia (daughter of John Hoskins Shearman) to obtain some information regarding his grandmother Sarah. In a very tactful reply Julia wrote: "I wish I could say anything which would give you pleasure or interest. As I look back I can only feel sorry for her. Your grandfather's three happy years were with his second wife of whom I need not speak as you knew her well".

Charles James Shearman was born in Rotherham, but followed in his father's footsteps and became a Physician in London. He was associated with University College and the Westminster Hospital. At the age of 29 he married Tryphena Jane Hodge, who was about 10 years his junior and came from the London area. The wedding took place on 12th May 1857 in Hampstead Parish Church. They subsequently moved to Sheffield and Charles James Shearman became a Physician at the Sheffield General Hospital. Their first child was a son, Percy Edward, who was born on 7th April 1858, at 58 Fargate, Sheffield: Fargate was situated in the centre of Sheffield but none of the original houses exist owing to city centre development. Ernest was their second child, born only one year later, also at 58 Fargate, Sheffield. Ernest and Percy were both baptised at St. Philip's Church, Sheffield by the Revd M. Livesey, Percy on 23rd June 1858 and Ernest on 12th July 1859: unfortunately that church no longer exists. At the time of the 1861 census, the family was living in Surrey Street, Sheffield, which is also in the centre of the city.

Percy Edward Shearman

On 16th November 1864, when Ernest was just 5½ years old, his father, aged only 37, died of pulmonary tuberculosis at Fryerning, Essex and was buried nearby at Ingatestone. His mother appears then to have moved back to London and in 1871 was living in Hampstead with her widowed mother.

Tryphena Shearman remarried on 5th December 1877 at St. George's Church, Hanover Square, London. Her second husband was a widower, Dr. Charles Atkinson, who had been in partnership with her first husband. He died shortly after the marriage but she survived until 14th August 1907 and died at her then home, Byrnelmscote, in Winchester. Percy Edward Shearman had been a witness at the remarriage which had been conducted by the Revd Thomas Smith, Vicar of Walkley, Sheffield. An anomaly in their marriage certificate gives Tryphena's middle name as Jeannie but she has signed her name as Jane.

Percy too was to become a Physician, but on 12th January 1884 at the early age of 25 he died of tuberculosis at Davos Platz, Switzerland. He had qualified at University College Hospital in 1880-81 and lived for about two years in The Grove, Wimbledon, Surrey. He became the Resident Clinical Assistant at the Consumption Hospital, Brompton. It is probable that he contracted tuberculosis there and went to Switzerland in hope of recovery. A family feud at the time of his death meant that the two brothers were not on speaking terms. It may even be that their mother's remarriage to Dr. Atkinson so many years previously started the dispute between Percy and Ernest.

Ernest Charles Shearman however decided not to follow the family tradition but to train as an architect. In 1876, at the age of 16 he was articled to Charles Barry (1823-1900), the son of Sir Charles Barry, architect of the Houses of Parliament. In 1877 he is recorded as attending the Royal Academy schools and later the Architectural Association, where he studying under Street and Norman Shaw. In 1881 he was living with his mother in the Wimbledon area.

On 18th August 1885 Shearman married Marian Catherine McGowran in the parish church of St. Mary at St. Briavels in Gloucestershire: the service was conducted by the vicar, the Revd William Taprell Allen, whom Shearman was later to commemorate in the stained glass east window for the church. At

Ernest Charles Shearman

the time of his marriage Ernest was 26, described himself as an architect and resided in the parish of Holy Trinity, South Wimbledon, Surrey. Marian was aged 25, and had resided in the Parish of St. Briavels in the Forest of Dean, which was her family home. She was born there on 25th June 1860, the daughter of Francis and Maria Eliza McGowran. She had attended Art College in Wimbledon and it is most probable that she and Ernest met while they were both living in that area.

Ernest and Marian had four children. The first was a daughter, born at 1, Dorset Road, Merton on 18th January 1887 and named on her birth certificate Ethel Margaret, which was changed to Elsie Margaret after registration. She was always known as Elsie Margaret, the name that appears both on her Will and death certificate as well as her letters. She remained single, died on 14th March 1969 and was buried in her parents' grave in Winchester. It is because of Elsie that so much of this history has been compiled, as she kept a great deal of material, which has now been carefully retained by her niece

Shearman Family Group
Back row: 1&2 not family, 3 Elsie Margaret, 4 Charles Edward Gowran.
Seated: Ernest Charles & Marian Catherine.
Front row: Jeane Evelyn & John Kinder Gowran.

Jeane Duffey, who inherited it.

In 1888 Shearman left his position with Sir Charles Barry and accepted employment as the architect to the Buenos Aires Great Southern Railway, which was then entering into a substantial period of expansion, with many new lines. He and his wife and daughter went to South America for about three years. Besides a number of railway buildings in Argentina, Shearman was also responsible for a number of ecclesiastical and domestic buildings. The railway stations are believed to still exist and are described as being very English, but none of the few books available in English on the railways appears to portray them.

The Shearmans' second child was a son, Charles Edward Gowran, born 1st May 1889, in Banfield, Argentina. He was subsequently baptised on 14th September 1889 at Holy Trinity Church, Lomas de Zamora, in the Province of Buenos Aires. He died on 10th July 1968 aged 79.

Shearman was closely associated with Holy Trinity Church, Lomas de Zamora, which was built in what was then a railway centre with an English presence. Not only was his son Charles baptised there, but he was involved as architect when the enlargement of the church became urgently necessary in 1890. Shearman added the chancel, vestry and organ chamber. The total work cost over $11.000 and the builder was

Elsie Margaret Shearman.

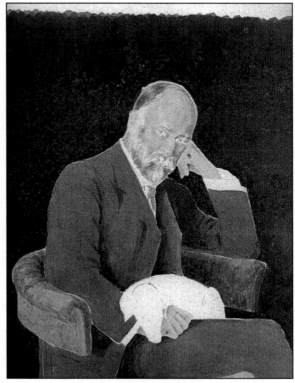

Ernest Charles Shearman – painting by Elsie Margaret.

Mr. J. Pollard. The additions were dedicated by the Bishop on 15th June 1890 and at the same time he blessed the font. This church was designed to be in the Anglo-Catholic tradition and remained so. It is clear that Shearman himself was within that tradition, but it is not clear how or when he became involved in it. The parish priest at Holy Trinity at that time was the dynamic and committed Anglo-Catholic, the Revd. Arnold Theophilus Biddulph Pinchard. In 1892 he became a Canon of Port Stanley Cathedral in the Falkland Islands, but in 1895 he returned to England for the sake of his wife's health and became vicar of St. Jude, Hill Street, Birmingham, where he was later to have further dealings with Shearman.

The Shearmans returned to England in 1891. On 13th June 1892 Ernest was elected an Associate of the RIBA after passing the examination, an important step in his career.

Following Shearman's return to England he was appointed resident architect under Colonel Robert W. Edis in the work of rebuilding Sandringham.[1] The upper parts of the House had been damaged by fire in 1891. At the behest of Princess Alexandra he did extensive work and a second storey was subsequently added. As architect in residence he knew her well enough to be invited to accompany her skating. On one occasion he fell and broke his nose and her remark was that "she thought it could only improve it".

In December 1892 Princess Alexandra presented him with a large signed photograph of herself which Shearman describes in extravagant terms to his wife in a letter from Sandringham dated 23rd December 1892.

He obviously felt extremely honoured and proud to have received this gift from the Princess and insisted that his wife should take care of the photograph and also "get a frame which was worthy of it". The tone of the letter to his wife concerning the gift of the photograph was boastful, teasing and commanding all at the same time.

There are also terms of endearment in the letter, where he addresses his wife as "my dear old darling" and describes his children aged five and three as "chicks", to whom he sends love and kisses. He was known to his wife by the nickname Erna.

Princess Alexandra's personal generosity was also extended to a gift of a beautiful grand piano. It is interesting to note that St. Gabriel, Noel Road, Acton, which was built between 1929 and 1931, possesses two very fine terracotta panels which were formerly in Sandringham Church, Norfolk and were given to them in 1930: they may perhaps have been presented to Shearman at the same time.

---

[1] Contact with the Estate Office at Sandringham and also the Archivist at Windsor Castle has not revealed any records of this connection.

THIS IS TO CERTIFY THAT

Ernest Charles Shearman,

(Buenos Aires) Kingston House Winchester,

Having passed the Qualifying Examination established in 1882, was elected,

on the thirteenth day of June 1892,

ASSOCIATE
OF THE ROYAL INSTITUTE OF BRITISH ARCHITECTS,

Founded in the Year of Our Lord, One thousand eight hundred and thirty-four, and afterwards constituted, under Royal Charters granted by King William the Fourth and Queen Victoria, a Body Politic and Corporate for the general advancement of Architecture, and for promoting and facilitating the Acquirement of the knowledge of the various arts and sciences connected therewith.

IN WITNESS whereof, the Common Seal has been hereunto affixed, at a Meeting of the Council, held at No. 9, Conduit Street, Hanover Square, London, this twenty-fifth day of July 1892.

_____ *Chairman of the Meeting.*

_____ *Member of Council.*

_____ *Member of Council.*

William H. White
The Secretary of the Royal Institute.

_____ *Honorary Secretary.*

Registered Serial No. *232*.

This Certificate is held subject to annual notification of its renewal, and under the conditions of By-law 24.

Associate RIBA Diploma.

Shearman's closeness to Princess Alexandra also seems to be apparent in that she acknowledged his letter when she was widowed. It is regrettable that the part of Sandringham that Shearman built for the King was pulled down some years ago, probably about 1970.

The Shearman's third child, a son, Alec Brooke, was born on 26th December 1893 at Tryphena Atkinson's home, Kingston House, Hyde Street, Winchester. It is very probable that he was named after Princess Alexandra, as Ernest was working on Sandringham House only days before Alec's birth and had just received the present and a signed photograph from the Princess. However, sadness was to enter the Shearmans' life, as Alec developed a sarcoma of the kidney and died of asthenia on 10th February 1896 at the tender age of three, with his father by his side. It is most strange that little Alec's birth certificate gives his Christian names as Alec Brooke, but on his death certificate he was registered in the name of Alec Arnold Wilkie.

Alec's death was the third of the tragic premature deaths which were to affect Shearman during his life. His father and brother had both died early of tuberculosis and the death of his child at this young age would have been the final blow to a weaker man. However within the next decade, when in his forties, he had the strength to embark on the beginning of the part of his career for which we mainly remember him, his church building, which is described in detail in the succeeding chapters.

At the time of Alec's death the family, for professional reasons, were living in Newmarket, Suffolk. It was on the recommendation of the Prince of Wales (later Edward VII) that after the success of his work at Sandringham he was asked to undertake the restoration of Sir Henry McCalmont's seat, Cheveley Park, near Newmarket. The family lived initially in Cheveley Road, Newmarket and then in 1904 moved to Westwood House, Exning, Cambridgeshire, but very near Newmarket. It was also during this period that he carried out work for the so-called "colony" erected at Chalfont St. Peter, Buckinghamshire for epileptics, which was expanding very rapidly in the period from 1894 to 1900 and involved substantial properties. Shearman's contribution was to design, in 1897, Eleanor House, a home for women on the site, now demolished. It is described as being an attractive red brick building with red roof tiles and half timbered oak gables.

By this time Shearman had a London office at 53, Berners Street, in the West End: much later he used an address at 2, Princes Square, in London W2.

The Shearmans' fourth child was a daughter, Joan Patricia, born 28th September 1900, in what was then her paternal grandmother's house, Byrnelmscote, Park Road, in Winchester. She, like her sister, remained single and died on 28th March 1973.

It was during this period in East Anglia, in 1900, that Shearman designed a new rectory for Brandon, on the Suffolk/Norfolk border. It was built on a piece of glebe land off the London Road at a cost of £2831 13s. 0d. The original contract was for £2100 and Shearman was paid £95 which made a total of £2195. The increase in the amount was due to alterations made by the architect after the contract was signed, omissions and additions by the architect, and the addition of stables. Shearman had been recommended for this work by the Bishop's Chaplain, the Revd. C. Bullock-Webster. The house stood in about an acre and a quarter of land with the more attractive rear of the house facing St. Peter's church. The rectory was of brick with a tiled roof. Out-buildings included a coach-house, stable for two horses, harness room and hay loft. The main property was on three floors with a cellar. The main ground floor rooms included the drawing room, dining room, kitchen, hall and study. The first floor had five bedrooms, two dressing rooms, bathroom and separate toilet. The second floor had three further bedrooms reached by a separate servants' staircase. The main staircase and the servants' staircase were joined by an interconnecting door. The cellar was divided into three sections by walls. Adjoining the kitchen was the scullery, larder, two areas for coals and the yard.

Brandon Rectory – elevation facing church.

Brandon Rectory.

Brandon Rectory.

Elevation . to . Church .

Ernest C. Shearman A.
53 Berners Street
Lond.

Brandon Rectory – elevation to church.

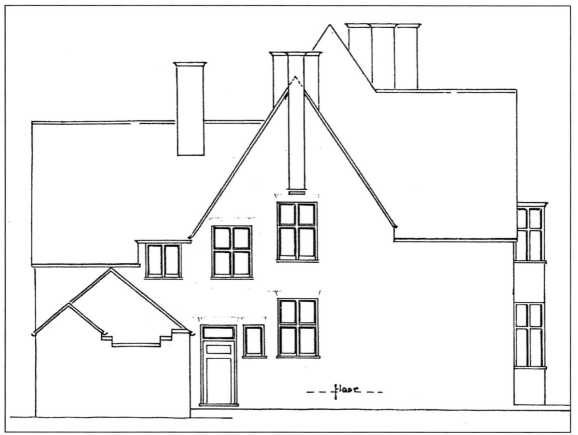

flare

Brandon Rectory – elevation to river.

11

Brandon Rectory – elevation front.

Brandon Rectory – elevation to avenue.

Brandon Rectory – ground floor.

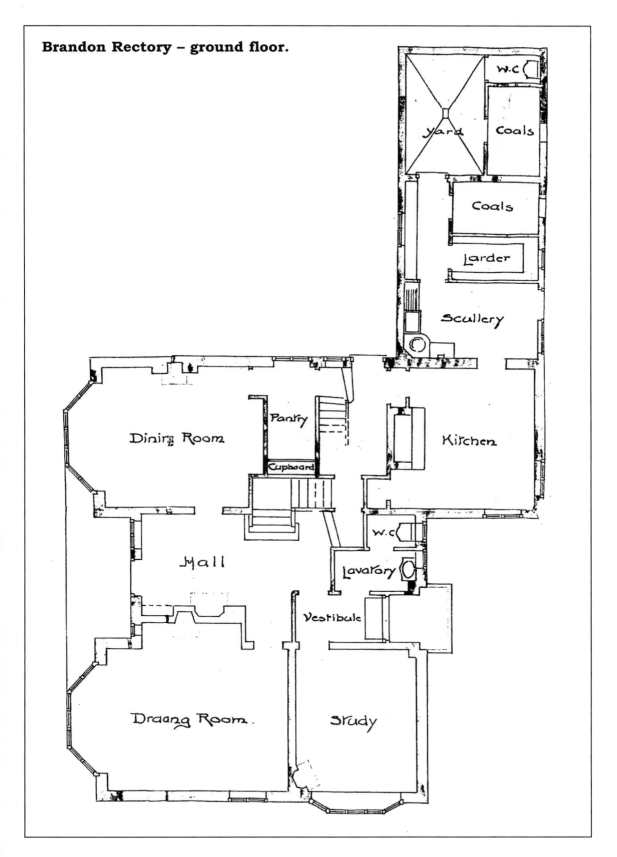

W.C

Yard

Coals

Coals

Larder

Scullery

Dining Room

Pantry

Cupboard

Kitchen

Hall

W.C

Lavatory

Vestibule

Draang Room.

Study

Brandon Rectory – first floor.

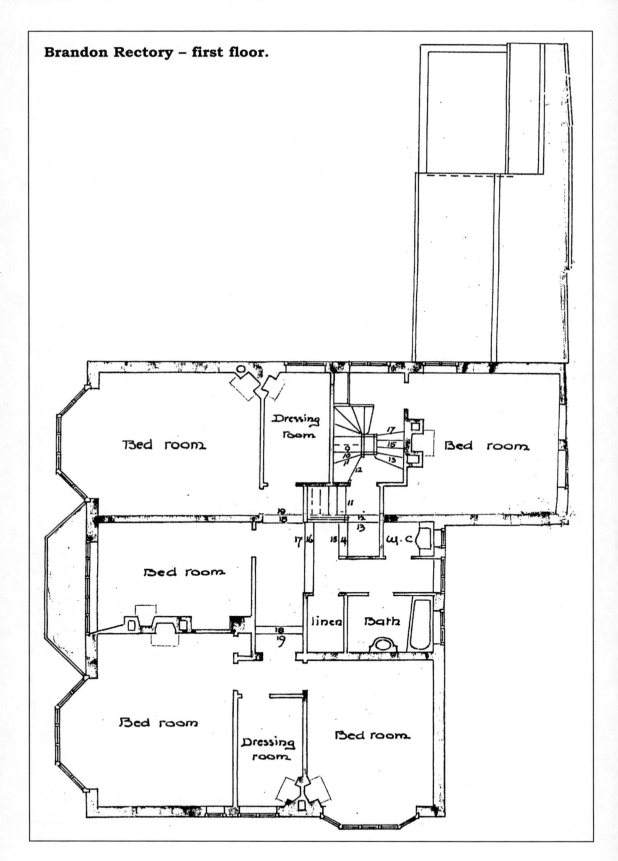

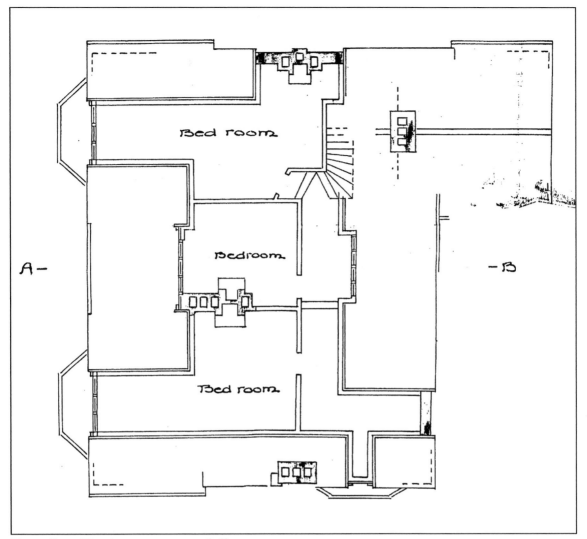

Brandon Rectory – second floor.

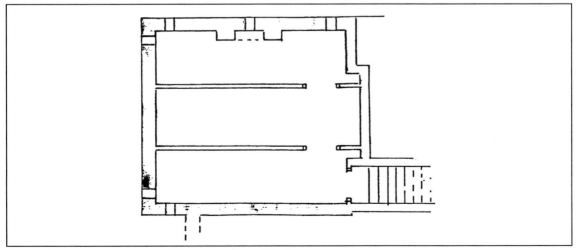

Brandon Rectory – cellars under dining room.

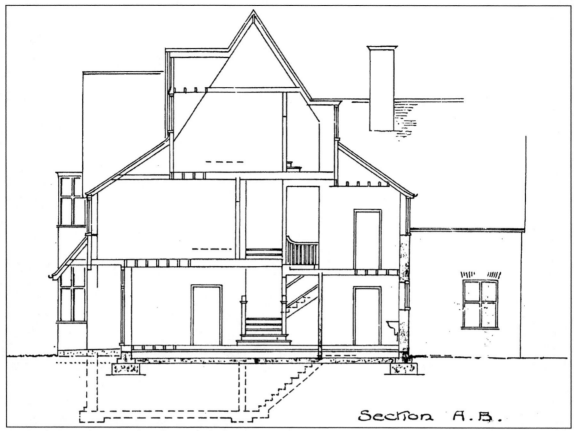

Brandon Rectory – section AB.

Manea Vicarage, Cambridgeshire.

Although no longer the rectory, the house is still in residential use.

It was in 1903-4 that a former public house was purchased for the incumbent at Manea, in the deepest Fens of Cambridgeshire and it was adapted by Shearman as a rectory.

In 1907, following the death of Ernest Shearman's mother Tryphena Atkinson, the family went to live at Byrnelmscote. He had designed this house for his mother and at her expense in about 1899, when she was living at Kingston House. Byrnelmscote has since been renamed Stapenhill by Mrs. C.M. Beckett when she took over the property in 1953. The house is situated on the north side of Park Road at the Worth Road end, opposite Park Close and between Courtenay Close and Abbotts Close.

The house comprises a two storey gable fronted detached property. The main front entrance door is on the west side of the south elevation and is approached from a small recessed porch. The property is traditionally constructed in solid load bearing stock brickwork under a pitched main roof covered in the original plain clay tiles. The front gable is rendered to the top section with a small timber casement with leaded lights. There are three dormer windows to the east roof slope with rendered fascia and dormer cheeks. The original timber casements with Georgian leaded lights have been retained throughout the accommodation and there are angular bay windows to the ground floor east elevation. The garden is accessed from flush double doors to the centre east elevation, on each side of these doors are small additional

Byrnelmscote, Park Road, Winchester – elevation facing tennis court.

Byrnelmscote, Park Road, Winchester – elevation from road.

Drawing of Byrnelmscote by CEGS & EMS for ECS Christmas present.

Vintage photographs of Byrnelmscote and its garden.

Vintage photograph of Byrnelmscote.

Byrnelmscote in the snow.

windows. There is a prominent chimney at the south-west corner and a short ridge stack between the middle and north dormers. Details of the west and north elevations are not known. The property does not have any out-buildings.

At the back of the house is a sunken lawn which during the occupancy of the Shearmans was a tennis court. This tennis court was a family venture and was always known as "Lorna Doone", because it was not level. The Shearmans were very fond of playing tennis and also for them no house was ever complete without a dog and probably a horse too. There used to be a paddock behind Byrnelmscote which extended to the parallel road. This area was sold and a house built on it at the end of the Second World War, in about 1946.

The interior of the house was noted for its dark panelling, the uncarpeted stairs and the beautifully vaulted cellars. It was decorated very much in the style of William Morris. It remained as the family home for the rest of Ernest Shearman's life.

Although Shearman had carried out some ecclesiastical work prior to his move to Winchester, it was after that move that his career flowered with the design of six London churches, details of which follow. These dominated the remainder of his professional life and he was working on the later projects until well into his 70s.

Shearman was involved in other activities apart from architecture

ECS with dog at Byrnelmscote.

and was particularly energetic in work on behalf of ex-members of the fighting forces. He was a member of the Council and Executive Committee of the Officers' Association and also the Committee of the Officers' Association Employment Bureau. Until his health prevented him, he attended daily for many years at the offices of this Association. He worked indefatigably on behalf of unemployed and disabled officers. This is a part of his life which is not pursued in detail in this work and it is not clear what drew him to it.

In the *Hampshire Chronicle and General Advertiser for the South and*

ECS with dog at Byrnelmscote.

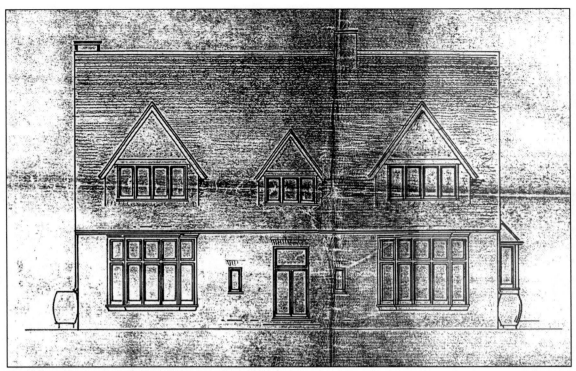

Byrnelmscote South East elevation.

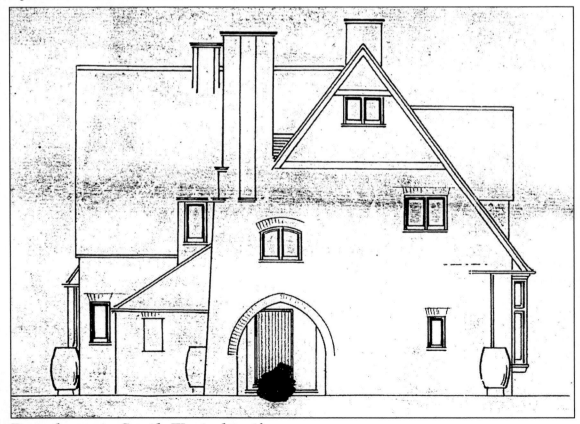

Byrnelmscote South West elevation.

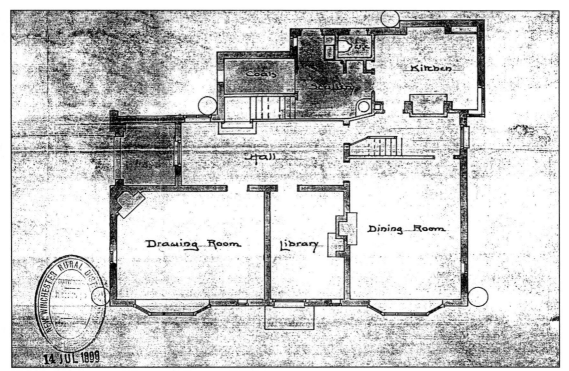

Byrnelmscote Plan of Ground Floor.

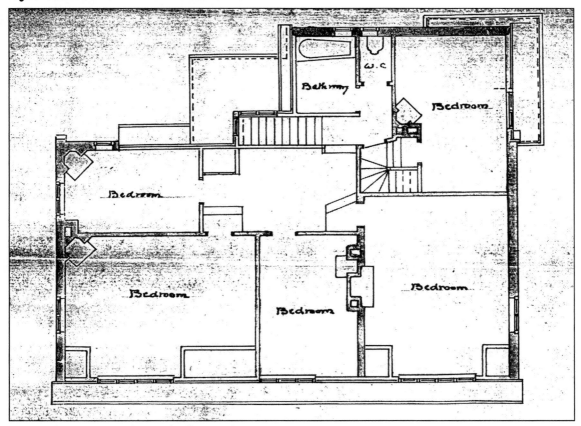

Byrnelmscote Plan of First Floor.

23

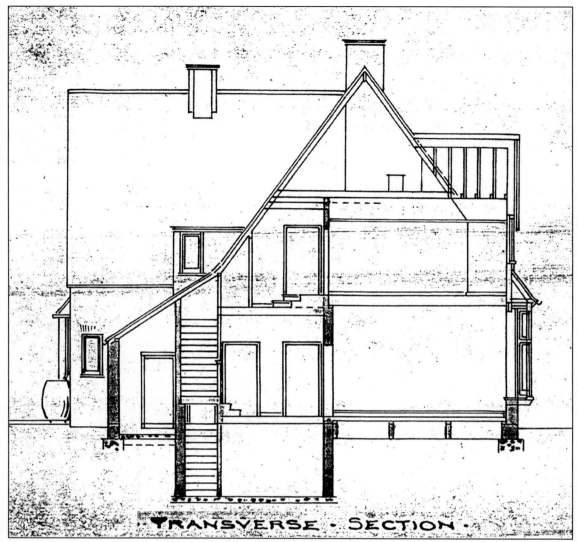

Byrnelmscote Transverse section.

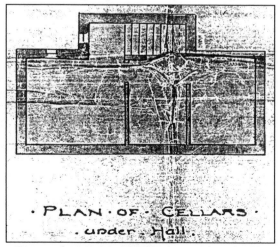

Byrnelmscote Cellars under hall.

24

St Bartholomew, Hyde Street, Winchester.

St Bartholomew, Hyde Street, Winchester.

West of England dated 22nd April 1939 it is stated in his obituary that Shearman was also a member of the Committee of the Incorporated Church Building Society. If this is so he had quite a humble position because in his negotiations with them over the applications for grants, he took a very subservient stance when corresponding with the architects Caroe and Passmore.

The ageing Shearman, in his correspondence to Father Hillier at St. Silas Church in October 1937, wrote that he suffered from intermittent episodes of asthma and had indeed visited the doctor that month with this condition. He also mentioned in the same letter that, owing to a fall down a staircase, his right knee would have to remain in plaster of Paris for two months.

Ernest Shearman died two weeks before his 80th birthday, on Monday, 17th April 1939 at his home, which was "Byrnelmscote" Park Road, Winchester. The cause of death was: I (a) Uraemia, (b) Chronic Nephritis, (c) Enlarged Prostate; II Myocarditis.

His funeral was at St. Bartholomew's Church, Hyde, which is in King Alfred Street, Winchester, on 21st April 1939. The service was conducted by the vicar, the Revd. W.R. Parr. During the service the 23rd Psalm was said and the Vicar read Revelations Chapter V as the lesson, which would have been especially significant at that time.

Shearman's favourite hymn *Praise, my soul, the King of Heaven* was sung. It would seem that that hymn was as appropriate for Shearman then, as it is now, as these are the sentiments which he would wish to convey, even today, in his architectural church work.

The interment took place at Magdalen Hill Cemetery, Winchester. Representatives were present from St. Barnabas, Temple Fortune and wreaths were received from the people of St. Matthew's Church, Wimbledon as well as from the Revd. and Mrs. Napier Whittingham.

Shearman's grave is unmarked and is known only by its plot no. U2/84. His wife died on 25th January 1953, aged 92, and is buried with him, as is his daughter, Elsie Margaret. A letter dated 18th May 1955 from his son, Charles to his daughter Elsie indicates that there should be a gravestone. He states that the inscription should be engraved and black enamel finish at 11/- per dozen letters and suggests that it should say "IN LOVING MEMORY OF ERNEST CHARLES SHEARMAN AND MARIAN CATHERINE HIS WIFE. 1859 – 1939 and 1860 – 1953." There was also to be a Portland stone kerbing.

The Shearman line was to continue through his only living son, Charles Edward Gowran Shearman, who married Evelyn Winifred White on 15th December 1924 at Christ Church, Mayfair, London.

They had two children – John Kinder Gowran Shearman and Jeane Evelyn Duffy, née Shearman, who have both kindly assisted in providing much information for this biography.

Watercolour of Marian Catherine Shearman painted by Elsie Margaret.

Artistic and medical traits have flowed though this family. The artistic trait has mainly followed the female side of the family whereas the medical trait seems mainly to be on the male side. Shearman's wife Marian attended Art College in Wimbledon and it also appears that his daughter Elsie must have been an accomplished artist, if the portrait of her mother can be taken as an example. She also started a watercolour painting of her father which is sufficiently finished for a good impression to be gained, luckily it is only the family pet sleeping on his lap which is totally incomplete. She also turned her hand to designing religious subjects, very skilfully portraying the Blessed Virgin Mary holding a lily in her left hand and a crozier with a symbolic crown of thorns crook in her right hand. Jeane Evelyn Duffy was to follow in her grandmother's footsteps and receive her artistic training at the same College in Wimbledon. John Kinder Gowran Shearman was to become a distinguished professor of Fine Arts at Harvard [2] and subsequently

[2] Very little indeed has been written about Shearman, but in L.R. Jones and L.C. Matthew *Coming About...A Festschrift for John Shearman* (Harvard University Art Museums, 2001) there is a short article by C.D.H. Row entitled *The London Churches of Ernest Charles Shearman: St. Silas the Martyr, Anglo-Catholicism and the Modern Gothic Tradition.*

three of his children have taken up artistic professions, whereas the fourth has followed in the footsteps of Edward James, Charles James and Percy Edward and taken up medicine.

However, Shearman's first son Charles followed neither of these family lines, but took a career in the army. At the time of his father's death he was living in York as Colonel C.E.G. Shearman, DSO, MC, but he later rose to the rank of Brigadier.

Shearman's granddaughter states that he was a man of very high ideals and moral standards. He was also not motivated by pecuniary gain and was quite unworldly about money. It is known that he did not charge to design the altars of his churches. Unfortunately his lack of interest in financial rewards caused the family to suffer some pecuniary embarrassment.

This belief of a granddaughter for her grandfather does bear some contrast with his own daughter's opinions. It appears that during the years when he worked and lived mainly in London he visited Winchester less frequently as the years progressed. It also seems likely that there were other attractions in London and that his daughter Joan in particular disapproved of "his women", whereas a letter from him to Elsie at the time made it seem quite normal. It is thought that this behaviour may have lost him a knighthood and greater recognition, but he would have looked upon such an idea with contempt.

In possible reply to his critics and an indication of his own feelings Shearman, on 13th December 1925, wrote to his daughter Elsie Margaret and sent her these few lines of verse by Cresswell, who he describes as Leader of the Labour Party in South Africa and a good man, not out for himself.

The man who fears to take his stand alone,
But follows where the greatest number tread,
Should hasten to his grave beneath a stone;
The great majority of men are dead.

APPENDIX

Letter from Ernest Charles Shearman to his wife Marian from Sandringham, dated 23rd December 1892:

"My dear old darling,

> *You will be proud of your hub now.*
> *The Princess has given me another proof of her Royal appreciation.*
> *She sent for me today and came to me in the drawing room. Again said how pleased she was with the work near her room –*

afterwards "I want to give you my portrait with a little Christmas present." Her Royal Highness then said a few more sweet things – and gave me her hand as she said good bye for Christmas.

This morning I was out by the lake just getting ready for a sketch when I saw the young Princesses coming towards the iron gate.

Princess Victoria leading by some two hundred yards.

I opened the gate for her and was duly thanked. When through the gate Her Royal Highness pulled up to say a few words to me, asked me if I was going to sketch. I said I was anxious to obtain a rough sketch from the lake, as the view was such a pretty one.

The wintry boughs against the sky and the brick gables.

She thought it a very pretty view – always did.

Further said "I suppose you are nearly finished now". "You have been very quick". – Then Princess Maud came up – bows exchanged and they were off again.

They both look very well on horseback.

Now for the description of my new treasures.

Lovely pearl studs. Three of them in Russian (?) case.

Aren't you jealous!! Such beauties – one pearl to each stud.

Wasn't it good of her.

I can't describe the way they were given – only the Princess can do these things, and it was done in her own way.

The photograph is delightful – full length, evening dress – or court dress (no – there are no feathers) with coronet of diamonds, such a beauty.

Now aren't you happy. I'm in the seventy and seventh heaven now. Get me a temporary frame for it.

White if you can, if not white – of oak.

But let it be good of its kind.

I don't want the picture spoilt, and everybody will want to see it.

It is signed of course, "Alexandra" –

Exact size of portrait 18" x 12½".

I doubt if you will get this size so get a frame as near as you can to it.

We must get a good one – worthy of the picture, next week.

Bye, bye; hope to be with you at 4.15 p.m. Any change necessary I will wire.

Love to the Chicks and kisses

Yr. loving

Erna"

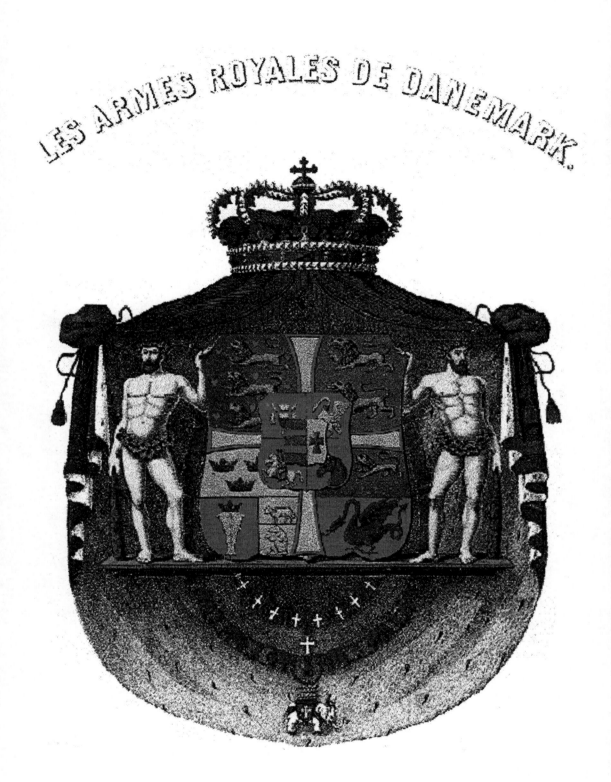

Document depicting the Danish Royal Arms which Shearman requested from Princess Alexandra possibly to use as guide for a memorial window.

SHEARMAN'S SIX LONDON CHURCHES:
AN OVERVIEW

After his institutional work at about the turn of the century, Shearman devoted himself more and more to the subject of church architecture and so started the period of his life when he was to design the six London churches, as well as being asked to assist in restoration and addition work in others. His churches were described in 1939 as having a simplicity and dignity which was uncommon but striking. They remain as a practical memorial to a man who had few equals in the architectural expression of the Christian belief and in the historical knowledge necessary to his art. His work can perhaps be seen as almost the final flowering of the last phase of the Gothic Revival. The later churches were certainly amongst the last to be constructed along those principles and to that extent they are backward looking.

In the period 1890 to 1900 the suburban churches of J.E.K. and J.P. Cutts were described as dull, but with the intention that they should be beautified in the future. Shearman inherited this outlook and so he perpetuated the ethos of the plain church, just affordable by the impoverished congregations who had packed their mission churches during the previous decade. Furnishings and ornaments were bought by the congregation who saved their farthings until the fittings we now admire could be added. The demand for originality was suppressed during the war years and Shearman produced his six churches in a uniform style, probably from the same blueprint but with variations as requested by the local people and by the site.

The six London churches chronologically are:-

St. Matthew, Durham Road, Cottenham Park, Wimbledon, SW20.
   This was built about 1910, and was destroyed during the Second World War on 29th June 1944. None of the original church survives. This church was rebuilt by J. Sebastian Comper.
St. Silas the Martyr, St. Silas Place, Kentish Town, NW5.
   Built 1911 to 1913.
St. Barnabas, Pitshanger Lane, North Ealing, W5.
   Built 1914 to 1916.
St. Gabriel, Noel Road, Acton, W3.
   Built 1929 to 1931.
St. Barnabas, Cranbourne Gardens, Temple Fortune, NW11.
   Built 1932 to 1934 and completed by Romilly B. Craze in 1962.
St. Francis of Assisi, Great West Road, Osterley, Isleworth.
   Built 1933 to 1935.
Shearman wrote of St. Silas: "The Church is designed on the

Basilican model with wide nave affording the whole congregation an uninterrupted view of the Sanctuary and Pulpit; the Altar being the centre of the Apse". This description equally applies to all the churches and shows the philosophy behind the construction.

The five London Churches still in existence are all situated north of the Thames. Superficially they all display a similarity, which the editors of *Pevsner* helpfully describe as Mediterranean Gothic. Christopher Row[1] indeed compares the spatial composition of St. Silas with that of Sta. Croce in Florence. They are all brick buildings without spires or towers, although in some cases they are known to have been designed to have towers. They all have an eastern apse and all have bands of stone string courses that are placed at various levels, which can either be in relation to the high lancet windows or at lower levels.

Less obvious, but with its symbolic meaning to Shearman, is the cruciform volume of the buildings. The churches have short cross transepts, but these are only evident at the clerestory level. Internally it is apparent that the transepts do not exist at ground level.

The lancet windows of the apse vary in subtle ways. St. Silas and St. Barnabas, Temple Fortune have five single lancets, St. Barnabas, Pitshanger Lane has five paired lancets, while St. Gabriel and St. Francis of Assisi have seven single lancets.

The two earlier churches, St. Silas and St. Barnabas, Pitshanger Lane both have ambulatory arcades encircling the apse, whereas this has been abandoned in the later churches. St. Gabriel does not have an ambulatory arcade, but does have recesses in the apse wall which give the impression of an arcade. In St. Francis, what would have been the arch leading to the ambulatory, has become the entrance to the chapels. In St. Barnabas, Cranbourne Gardens there is no ambulatory arch, but there is a lady chapel to the south of the chancel. In St. Gabriel the arch which would have led into the ambulatory on the south side of the chancel leads into the lady chapel and on the north side there is a deep recess where the arch would be.

All the churches have narrow passage aisles to the north and south of the nave. In all but St. Barnabas, Cranbourne Gardens the piers and their bases have a remarkable similarity, although the degree to which the arch is pointed does vary slightly. The nave of St. Barnabas, Cranbourne Gardens was completed by R.B. Craze many years after Shearman's death. The piers here appear more slender due to their plainness – lack of fluting and lack of bases. They extend without decoration to the ground.

Except for St. Silas they all have either one or two rose windows.

---

[1] See Row in *Coming About*, op.cit., p351.

St. Silas however does have a half rose window hidden away near the south porch.

The rose window is the most extraordinary feature of all Shearman's churches. Why was he so fascinated by them? Why is the rest of his style so austere when the roses are so fine, delicate and so intricate? Shearman obviously loved round windows! Each one is unique and most have flowing tracery. None were spoilt by stained glass, which would have hidden the flowing patterns made by the leading. His fascination started with St. Matthew and continued until its climax at St. Francis of Assisi.

At St. Matthew, the rose window, known as the Bishop's Eye, was set in the south transept wall as at St. Gabriel and was also of a very similar design. It was divided into four sections by a mullion and transom.

St. Silas does not have a traditional style rose window, but there is a semi-circular window on the south side of the apse. It is divided by

West rose window St Barnabas, Pitshanger Lane.

33

Half rose window at St Silas, Kentish Town on south elevation.

Interior view of part of half rose window at St Silas, Kentish Town.

Half rose window at St Silas, Kentish Town from south chapel.

Round roof window in St Francis chapel (now the sacristy), St Silas, Kentish Town.

Rose window by Comper in the rebuilt St Matthews, Wimbledon.

Rose window south chapel St Barnabas, Pitshanger Lane.

Rose window south chapel St Barnabas, Pitshanger Lane.

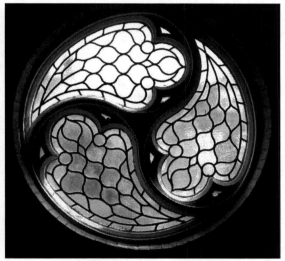

Circular window in upper room St Barnabas Pitshanger Lane.

a mullion and shows the rudiments that originated at St. Matthew's and were to be followed in the rest of his churches. However there is a rose/round window in the roof of the sacristy. This window has stained glass and depicts seven angels.

At St. Barnabas, Pitshanger Lane, the lady chapel, which is to the south of the chancel, has a six-petal window with fine tracery leading and almost entirely plain glass except for the slightest pastel blue tinge in a few of the panes. The west wall has a large eight-petal window traversed by cruciform mullion and transom. In the upper room, which was designed in 1936 and built by Shearman above the sacristy, is a small tripartite window with the typical swirling leading

Rose window south elevation St Gabriel, North Acton – only fully visible from outside church.

Architect drawing rose window south elevation St Gabriel, North Acton.

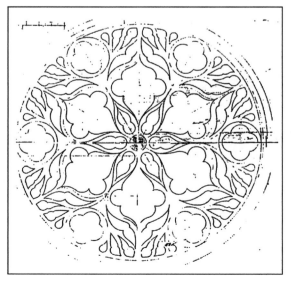

Architect's drawing for a rose window, west elevation, St Gabriel, North Acton.

Rose window St Barnabas, Temple Fortune south chapel.

Rose window St Barnabas, Temple Fortune west end but not by ECS.

Rose window west end St Francis of Assisi, Isleworth.

Rose window west end St Francis of Assisi, Isleworth.

which can be seen in the larger windows. The design of this window was previously used at St. Francis of Assisi.

At St. Gabriel, set in the south transept wall is a four-petal rose window with cruciform mullion and transom. This window is not fully visible from inside the church as it is in the false transept, partly hidden by a central pillar. Only about half the window can be seen from any one position inside the church, so its full glory has to be seen from the roadside and because the mullion and transom are fairly sturdy, the rest of the stone work is seen to be particularly fine. Shearman also designed a six-petal rose window for the west end of the church. The design shows this window was to be without mullion or transom and of massive size. However it was never built, but it does appear to be similar in design to the window in the lady chapel at St. Barnabas, Pitshanger Lane.

At St. Barnabas, Cranbourne Gardens, in the south transept lady chapel there is a west facing eight-petal window which was completed during Shearman's lifetime. The stonework here is fairly heavy and the leading design unusual in that it incorporates a six strand halo in the outer petals and a narrower four strand halo in the inner petals. In the west wall of the nave is a "six plus six" petal window which is much more geometrically shaped than any of Shearman's other windows. The leading is only of squared panels and atypical of Shearman. It is unlikely that it could be attributed to him. This window was not installed during Shearman's lifetime, but by R. B. Craze when the church was finally completed in 1962, as neither money nor expertise were available at this time to do justice to Shearman's original plans.

At St. Francis of Assisi, in the west wall of the nave, is arguably Shearman's finest architectural achievement, a fine rose with eight petals, four pointed and four round. The stone work is delicate and the leading intricate and exciting with no mullion or transom to spoil the effect. Each panel has its own special design and makes a totally balanced window. Is this Shearman's most perfect work? There are also two small round windows situated under the eaves of both the south and the north transepts. It is a tripartite design very similar to that later used at St. Barnabas, Pitshanger Lane.

The apse roof of the three earlier remaining churches is supported by a framework in the shape of a half cartwheel. St. Barnabas, Cranbourne Gardens has a vaulted ribbed roof and St. Francis has a painted panelled roof. St. Matthew's had a vaulted ribbed roof, with painted timber – almost identical to that at St. Barnabas.

Shearman strongly believed that the organ and choir should be at the west end of a church and that "the adoption of the eastern position [for a choir] has brought destruction to many a beautiful chancel..."2

Shearman was a real artist and his work was his vocation, even apart from his own religious convictions. He also had strong views regarding the foundation stones of his churches. He would not allow the inscription to be carved on the stone before it was laid and the foundation stone had to be the first stone that was laid and was to be placed directly upon the concrete foundation. They are found at the base of the chancel arch on the south side. It is noteworthy that the foundation stone at St. Barnabas, Pitshanger Lane is still without an inscription.

Three of the churches have low brick walls between the nave and the chancel. In St. Silas this wall has two steps along its length, whereas St. Gabriel has one and St. Francis has none. St Barnabas, Cranbourne Gardens has a low wooden screen incorporating the lectern and pulpit – all designed by Shearman. St. Barnabas, Pitshanger Lane only has a one-course stone wall.

The fonts of each church show a complete diversity and all have different origins and styles. Only St. Silas has a brick and stone font totally in the style of the rest of the church. Would Shearman have designed his other churches without fonts? It would seem unlikely. St. Barnabas, Cranbourne Gardens has an excuse as it was only completed well after Shearman's death and has a barrel-shaped font made of Portland stone with fishes round the base. St. Barnabas, Pitshanger Lane has an octagonal bowl, decorated with a floral design, on an octagonal pedestal that gradually widens to the base and is placed on an octagonal step. St. Gabriel has an octagonal font with shields and rosettes on the bowl and with statues in the niches round the pedestal. St. Francis has an almost plain octagonal font on a conjoined four pillar pedestal placed on two rectangular steps, which may be by Shearman.

Three of the churches have the same style of stations of the cross, from the same source, the Community of the Sisters of the Church, originally based in Kilburn and now at Ham. They have slight differences in appearance; those in St. Gabriel and St. Barnabas, Pitshanger Lane being in their original dark sepia colour, but those in St. Silas were later painted.

St. Barnabas, Cranbourne Gardens has a bronze art-deco aumbry with embossed vine leaves on the door and with an escutcheon in the shape of a bunch of grapes with pale purple stones over the lock. The aumbry is set in a panel of green marble. St. Francis has an almost identical aumbry which unfortunately has lost its escutcheon,

---

2 Letter from Shearman to the *Journal of the RIBA* Vol. 17, 1910 (p169).

but it does also have a small chrism safe below it; both are set in green marble.

Shearman's London churches are very similar in style and ideas. Shearman's austere architecture was specifically designed for elaborate furniture to be added. Nowhere demonstrates this better than St. Silas, where the interior of the church is blessed with its unique and fine furnishings.

In many of his architectural church works there are hidden meanings and Shearman wanted us to search for them. At St. Silas he put a large cross high up on the west wall with two lancet windows on either side to represent the Passion with Mary and the beloved disciple standing by. At St. Barnabas, Pitshanger Lane, in the lady chapel, he placed a small gallery with a stairway to heaven above it. Each of his churches has its false transepts representing the arms of Christ on the Cross and giving the churches a cruciform shape when seen from the air although not always apparent at ground level.

In September 1930, while Shearman would have been working on St. Gabriel's, Acton, he had requested his daughter Elsie to investigate for him the attributes or emblems of St. Gabriel. Shearman had thought that a trumpet was Gabriel's attribute, but Elsie was not able to confirm this for him in the books she had available.

At the time of his death Shearman was working on a panel for the High Altar at St. Barnabas Church, Temple Fortune, which is based on words from Revelation Chapter V. As was his custom, he was collaborating with the vicar of St. Bartholomew, Winchester, the Revd. W.R. Parr, to determine how the work should be done and to establish the correct symbolism.

It can be seen from these examples that Shearman was conscious of the symbolism he portrayed in each church and was anxious that it should be correct.

He was exceptional in that he designed most of the contents of each church, including details such as altar cloths, statuary and even Christmas cribs.

ST MATTHEW, WIMBLEDON

In 1895 a small iron church was built at the corner of Durham Road and Richmond Road, Wimbledon because it was felt that there was a need to build up an Anglo Catholic tradition in the area. By 1906 this church was far too small. It was decided that a more permanent church was needed and a building committee was formed. From the plans of five architects, the basilica design of Ernest C. Shearman was chosen at an estimated cost of £7,000.

The building of Shearman's church started on Ascension Day, 28th May 1908, when an ashen stake was driven into the ground from which the foundation measurements were taken. The building contractors were Messrs. James Burges & Sons, Wimbledon. Five weeks later the foundation stone was laid and on 10th July 1909 the new church was consecrated by the Bishop of Southwark, the Right Revd. Edward Stuart Talbot. By this date only the east end and one bay had been built to provide seating for 300.

After a substantial period in which only that part of the church was in use, on All Saints Day 1926 work recommenced and a further extension to the nave was completed by St. Matthew's Day, 21st

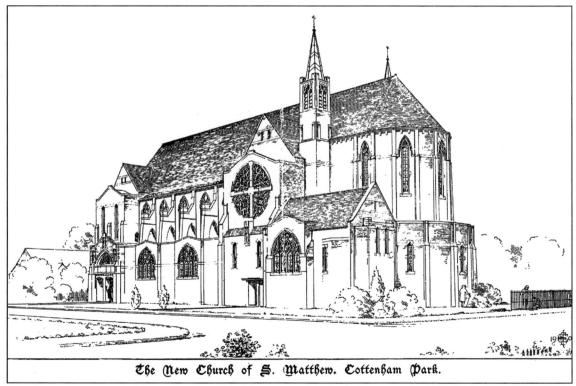

The New Church of S. Matthew. Cottenham Park.

Architect's drawing of the exterior.

: S:MATTHEWS.Church.
: WIMBLEDON :

Architect's drawing of the interior.

September 1927, but full completion of the west end and the turrets seems to have waited until 1929.

In 1935 the building was further enhanced by the installation of stained glass in the three central apsidal windows. The subject was the vision of St. John the Divine. At the top of the centre light was the figure of Our Lord, crowned and robed in a golden vestment, enthroned

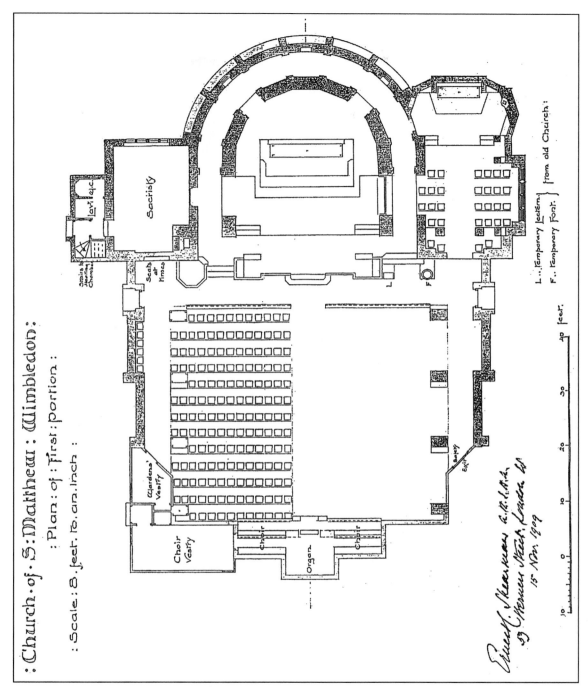

Architect's ground plan 1910.

upon the Great White Throne. One hand was raised in the attitude of blessing, the other holding the Book of the Seven Seals. Round about the throne and extending into the lights on either side was the rainbow "like unto an emerald". In the upper parts of each of the side windows was an angel holding a censer. Proceeding from the throne was the "River of the Water of Life, clear as crystal". On either side was the Tree

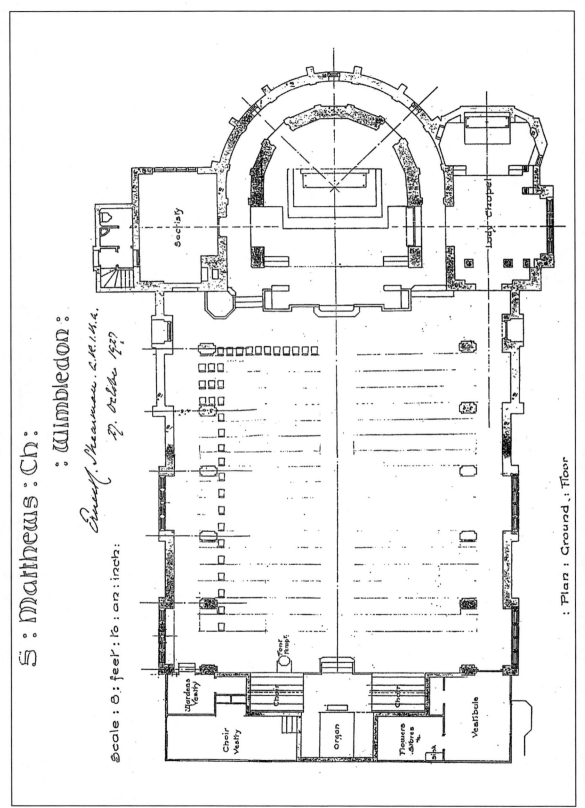

Architect's ground plan 1927.

Street scene with St Matthew, Wimbledon on the horizon.

St Matthew, Wimbledon 1910.

of Life bearing the twelve manner of fruits and spreading branches over all three lights. At the base of the windows were the words "The leaves of the Tree for the healing of the nations".

During this period, wooden figures of the Archangels St. Michael and St. Gabriel were installed high up on the corbels at each side of the entrance to the sanctuary, to left and right respectively.

During the Second World War, at about 8.30pm on the evening

St Matthew, Wimbledon, with turrets in 1929.

of St. Peter's Day, 29th June 1944, this beloved church was totally destroyed by a flying bomb and a devastating fire broke out in the ruins. Every effort was made to salvage as many vestments and ornaments as could be found.

The congregation of St Matthew's wanted to maintain their identity and continued, at the invitation of Christ Church Wimbledon, to have their own Sung Eucharist at 10 a.m., leaving the church by 11 a.m. to enable the usual Christ Church service of Matins to take place. For some months the daily eucharist took place in the sacristy, which had not been destroyed and which was located immediately beneath the north-east turret. The vestment chest was used as the altar. However, falling masonry from the turret threatened the worshippers so this privilege had to stop.

The charred reredos from the lady chapel was also saved and has been restored and repainted.

The church hall, adjoining the church, was also designed by Shearman and was also damaged on the evening of 29th June 1944, but in 1948 it was restored to be used as a temporary church and known as the Little St. Matthew's. Full rebuilding was carried out thereafter by Sebastian Comper and completed in 1956.

St. Matthew's, which was the fore-runner of all Shearman's

Interior east end 1909.

Interior east end 1929.

Interior east end 1929.

South passage aisle.

London churches, sets the pattern for his five other churches. Externally St. Gabriel's, Acton most resembles St. Matthew's in appearance. As with the other Shearman churches there was other planned building work that remained incomplete.

St Matthew's had an eastern apse and also an ambulatory passage. The aim of the design was to present the form of a basilica, invested with the traditional character of an English Parish Church with a wide open nave and narrow aisles, solely for passage. The whole congregation enjoyed an

Statue of St Gabriel, 1935.

uninterrupted view of the altar and pulpit. There were two-light clerestory windows in the nave (similar to St. Barnabas, Pitshanger Lane) and a pair of four-light windows along the south aisle. The lady chapel was located at the south-east corner and also had a four-light

After bombing, 1944.

After bombing, 1944.

After bombing, 1944.

window. The false transept on the south side had a rose window very reminiscent of St. Gabriel's with its broad mullion and transom. However, there were no plans for a west rose window.

This was Shearman's only church with turrets. These were located at the south-east and the north-east junctions of the nave and chancel. The south-east turret housed the bell and the north-east had two chimneys incorporated into the easternmost corners. The turrets were paid for by Mr. C.W. Robbins who was clerk of works for the church. The other Shearman churches were obviously designed with the possibility of having turrets, as vestigial mini-towers have been built up to lower roof level in each of them.

The main entrance was a south-west double porch, similar to that found at St. Barnabas, Pitshanger Lane, but here surmounted by three niches for statues. There was also a north porch and there were also plans to build a ceremonial entrance. No external statues had been placed in any of the niches outside the church before its destruction.

Internally the apse was designed with corbels between the lancet windows. There were five tall lancet windows in the apse. Between the chancel and the ambulatory were Gothic openings to north and south, but there was no opening behind the high altar as there is at St. Barnabas, Pitshanger Lane. The ceiling of the apse had timbered

Reredos from lady chapel.

Reredos from the lady chapel depicting the annunciation.

vaulting with spines from the lancet windows and was identical to the eastern section of that at St. Barnabas, Temple Fortune. It was painted red and gold with panels of blue with silver stars.

The chancel was reached by three steps from the nave and was divided from the sanctuary by two further steps, on one of which was located the altar rail. The high altar was a further three steps above that. Behind the high altar was a black marble gradine for the altar cross and candlesticks. There was an additional space behind the gradine for an altar-frontal chest. The sanctuary was decorated with a dorsal curtain and there was a tester above the high altar.

As at St. Gabriel's, the lady chapel was at the south-east corner of the church and it was there that the Blessed Sacrament was reserved in an aumbry.

The font was of stone with a fluted base and originated in the previous church.

Reredos from lady chapel.

The pulpit was designed by Shearman in stone and white brick and was incorporated into the north chancel arch with access from the ambulatory. It had an oak mantle which had an area scooped out to take a pocket watch to time the sermon. A tester was added later, but it was not a Shearman feature. Over the pulpit hung a picture of the crucifixion.

It appears that there were five bays in the nave, the most easterly being below the false transept. The west end had a mezzanine gallery that housed the organ. The vestry was located off the ambulatory on the north side.

The church was built mainly of brick but with stone facings. Externally Blue Staffords and internally Fletton bricks were used. It had a steeply pitched roof of Welsh green slates.

The main entrance to the church was situated at the south west corner of the church. Other entrances were below the south false transept rose window; at the east end of the north passage aisle and into the sacristy.

Reredos from lady chapel.

The rounded apse had three single lancet windows in the ambulatory and five single lancets at clerestory level. In the south false transept there was a rose window with mullion and transom (appearing to be identical to that at St. Gabriel). In the north false transept there were three single lancet windows at clerestory level. The nave had paired lancet clerestory windows to north and south. There was a four light window in the lady chapel and also similar windows in the second and fourth bays on the south side of the nave. Only the central three apse clerestory windows had stained glass (see previous details) – the designer and maker are not known.

The bays were broad Gothic arches with brick pillars (visually identical to St. Silas). The passage aisles were similarly so. Narrow gothic arches led into the ambulatory.

The apse was decorated with hexagonal shaped plaster plaques joined by beading. The plaques portrayed a bunch of grapes surrounded by a vine and vine leaves. They were arranged in vertical columns of four and in horizontal rows round the apse.

Reredos from the lady chapel depicting the nativity.

Boss from east wall decoration, 1929.

The vaulting of the apse ceiling contained an outer arc of shields bearing the symbols of various saints and along a central arc of plaques were portrayed the apostles surrounding a central boss of the Paschal Lamb. The overall design was identical to that found at St. Barnabas, Temple Fortune.

There was a tester over the high altar, painted in blue and gold with a radiant sun on its under-surface.

The fittings of St. Matthew's church were designed by John Hinds. The most important of these was the reredos incorporating carvings of four female Saints on each side of the Annunciation. This was surmounted by a carving of the Nativity. These items were saved from the bombed church. The main panel is now in the lady chapel of the present church.

St Matthew, Wimbledon by J.S. Comper.

St Matthew, Wimbledon by J.S. Comper.

The Saints on the reredos panel are from left to right St. Catherine of Alexandria with her wheel, St. Cecilia with a lyre, St. Anne with the child Mary holding a lily, St. Elizabeth of Hungary with her basket of flowers and on the other side of the Annunciation panel is St. Mary Magdalene with an alabaster box, St. Etheldreda of Ely with a model of the church of St. Matthew under her cope, St. Joan of Arc with a cross and sword and St. Margaret of Scotland holding a sceptre. The nativity panel now hangs on the west wall of the present church. St. Barnabas, Temple Fortune also commissioned Hinds to produce a reredos and altar.

Another important item saved from the Shearman church was the figure of the Archangel St. Michael which stood guard on a corbel at the entrance of the chancel and facing a similar statue of St. Gabriel.

The rugged cross and candlesticks from the High Altar were also saved, although badly tarnished by the fire which ensued after the Shearman Church was bombed.

Vicars of St. Matthew were as follows:-

1903	R. Rocksborough-Smith
1904	C. P. Fynes-Clinton
1916	F. M. McKeown
1917	W. C. Campling
1918	S. K. Anderson
1924	R. G. Morecombe
1928	D. F. Wilkinson
1931	F. C. Strother
1936	P. B. Hacker
1939	J. H. Jones
1945	John Yeend

APPENDIX

Copy of letter from Shearman to the Committee of the Incorporated Church Building Society.

Byrnelmscote,
Winchester.
12 May 1908

Dear Sir

St. Matthew's – Wimbledon

I have made a separate drawing showing the arrangement for the temporary west end.

The sacristy must serve for the choir till the west end is completed. The choir will be a small one. The organ also is small & will be brought from the iron temporary Church.

A cover & also a decent well will be provided for the font.

... well provided with entrances that I think the reference to increased entrances must be for the first ... before the three west end double doorways are built. [I am thinking of St. Paul's, Westminster Abbey, the Roman Cathedral of Westminster, All Saints Margaret Street, as support for this interpretation].

I have, therefore, added a door in the temporary west wall to meet this objection – not raised I might add, by the Local Authorities, who specifically asked for the width of doors & were content.

I have figured the thickness of walls on the ... and have increased the sacristy walls to 18 inches – but as regards the small part of the vestries which have walls 14 inches thick, I would point out that they have no weight to carry. It is a small matter, however & I will do what your Committee wish – if after this they still wish them increased in thickness.

Our brickwork bill is a heavy one, and I did not see the necessity of making walls with so little to do as thick as walls which have work to do.

The position of the font was a matter of no little thought.

Funerals would use the easternmost of the two large doors in the south porch – the west door would not be convenient for this purpose.

I hope the back rows of seats will be cleared during the week, so as to leave a fair open space at the west of the church, when completed.

Therefore, I assumed that the coffins & the bearers, or bier, would pass to the east of the font.

The late Mr. Pearson taught me not to put the font away in a corner.

It seems to me to occupy the best possible place as it is – but I shall be glad to listen to anything your very able Committee may say against my view.

Faithfully yours

Ernest C. Shearman

ST. SILAS THE MARTYR, KENTISH TOWN

Mission work began in this impoverished area of Kentish Town in 1877 with the appointment of the Revd. M.J. Sutton by the London Diocesan Home Mission. The first services were held out of doors, but later in local houses. A property which was originally 5, Preston Street was bought and became the site of the mission church. The Revd. P.R. Malony was appointed in 1882 and began the construction of the first church in 1884 to serve the needs of the area. This church, designed by C.L. Luck, was a simple structure in the Early English style, built of brick with stone facings. It seated 150, although the mission district had a recorded population of 5,566. This building now serves the function of a church hall and adjoins the new church which was built by Shearman in 1911-1913. The Revd. F.W. Bentley succeeded to the mission in 1892 and it was he who started to introduce a more ritualistic liturgy. In 1905 the mission received a bequest of approximately £7,000 from a Mr. Henry Howard Paul, a wealthy American resident in London. However the funds were not released for six years and it then fell to the Revd. G. Napier Whittingham, who had been appointed in 1907, to build the new church of St. Silas.

Father Napier Whittingham was an uncompromising Anglo-Catholic who was adept in raising money for his projects from a variety of wealthy benefactors. The release of the Paul estate funds allowed the building contract to be finally signed in October 1911. The architect appointed for the new church was Shearman, who had completed St.

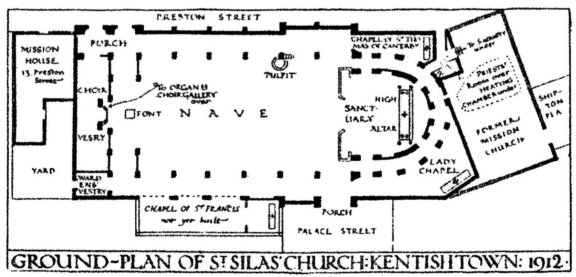

Ground plan drawn by Benjamin C. Boulter.

View in Preston Street

⋈—Existing small Mission Church.

Architect's drawing of exterior showing apse and north elevation.

Matthew, Wimbledon the previous year. From 1909-10 Shearman had close contact with Father Napier Whittingham and St. Silas, which is evident from his subscription to the monthly paper, mainly written and compiled by the vicar. Reference is made to his donations to the church funds, jumble sale and flowers for the mission church.

The foundation stone was laid on 16th December 1911 by Princess Marie Louise and was blessed by the newly appointed Bishop of Willesden, the Rt. Revd. William Perrin.

The consecration was announced in *The Building News*, 25th October 1912, in the following way:-

> "Kentish Town, N.W. – The new church of St. Silas-the-Martyr will be consecrated by the Bishop of London tomorrow (Saturday) afternoon. This church is planned as a basilica, having a wide nave, with aisles only for passages, so as to provide an

Interior showing Baldachino somewhat as it
will be when completed.

Architect's drawing of interior showing the baldacchino.

St SILAS' CHURCH
from SHIPTON PLACE
1913

Drawing by Benjamin C. Boulter towards the apse.

uninterrupted view of the altar at the east end. An ambulatory round the apse gives access to a small lady chapel in the south aisle, and the clergy vestry in the north. A larger chapel to the south of the nave will be built as soon as the cost can be met. The choir and organ occupy the west gallery, and room is afforded for stringed instruments and piano as well as organ. The west end also has an apse, necessitated by the rights of light of the windows of adjacent property. Both the eastern and the western apses rise to the full height of the main building. The architect is Mr. E. C. Shearman, A.R.I.B.A of Berners-street, W."

Foundation stone situated at the base of the chancel arch.

The church was consecrated, as promised in *The Building News,* on Saturday 26th October 1912 by the Bishop of London, the Rt. Revd. A.F. Winnington-Ingram in

St Silas, Kentish Town, from the Prince of Wales Road.

Procession in the 1920s in Palace Street (now St Silas Place).

Procession in the 1920s in Palace Street (now St Silas Place).

the presence of the Bishop of Willesden and Princess Marie Louise. The parish paper reported it as follows:

> "The architect almost lived in the church during the last fortnight, and thanks to his determination the church was sufficiently ready to be consecrated. But it was a near thing. At 11 a.m. on the day of consecration ... the church was full of scaffolding, without matting, without chairs, and the high altar not even in place. There was a small crowd of us waiting in the old church, longing to be useful the while the clock ticked near

Foundation stone for St Francis chapel.

South elevation.

North and west elevations.

Apse and north elevations.

to the fateful hour. At 12.30 p.m. we were allowed in and then we raced to lay the matting and set the chairs and every form we could lay our hands on, and went to work with a will. The baldachino was up and also the choir gallery, but both rather groggy about the supports, however we hoped for the best. Everything was ready by 2 p.m., and as the doors opened the workmen cleared away the scaffolding.

After the ceremony Princess Marie Louise held a reception in the old mission church, now the church room, at which both Bishops were present and many friends from all parts. Those present included Shearman, two Members of Parliament, the Rt. Hon. G.W.E. Russell and Rt. Hon. W.H. Dickinson, and 40 neighbouring clergy".

The chapel of St. Francis of Assisi, the building of which had been deferred, was begun in 1913. The foundation stone was laid on 25th July 1913 and it was consecrated on 1st November 1913.

In 1919 Shearman was commissioned to design a "Peace Memorial Porch" for the south entrance to the church. The design, illustrated in the May-June 1919 edition of the monthly paper, was considered as too ambitious for the church and was rejected. A second design of a double porch and separate calvary, illustrated in the

North elevation.

September-October 1919 edition, was accepted and added to the south entrance. The revised plans placed a calvary on a plinth on the right of the doorway. A stone statue of a centurion was placed above the doorway on the left and St. George and St. Joan of Arc were carved on either side of the door. The new work was consecrated on 2nd October 1920 by the Bishop of Willesden and Shearman was thanked in the parish paper for his "magnificent work".

Shearman, in an appeal for funds to build St. Silas, described his own work in the following way: "The church is designed on the basilican model with wide nave affording the whole congregation

South elevation showing the windowless St Francis chapel.

South entrance.

Apse.

North porch.

an uninterrupted view of the sanctuary and pulpit; the altar being the centre of the apse".

Neither Shearman's own description nor that printed in *The Building News* give full justice or adequate details of this church, although it can be regarded as a starting point to describe all Shearman churches.

St. Silas the Martyr was designed in Shearman's Mediterranean Gothic Style and was built between 1911 and 1913 by James Burges and Sons, of Wimbledon, who had recently completed Shearman's first church, St. Matthew, Wimbledon.

The main entrance is on the south side of the church and access is from St. Silas Place, a cul-de-sac off Prince off Wales Road. From this direction one gets

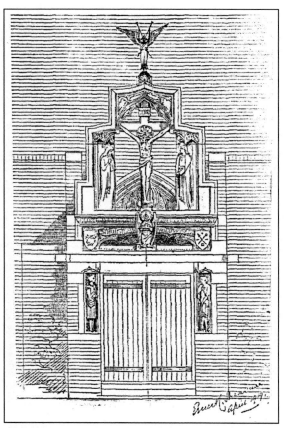

Rejected plan for War Memorial.

The War Memorial outside St. Silas-the-Martyr.

Accepted plan for War Memorial.

an overall view of the church. One is immediately aware of the eastern apse, the high pitched tiled roof, lack of spire or tower and also the narrow lancet clerestory windows, which are all typical of the style of Shearman. Also from this perspective the vestigial transepts are apparent. Below this is the double porch that was built onto the south transept in 1920. It is obvious that this is mainly a brick building with minimum of stone dressings strategically placed to add character to the church's exterior. Approaching the porch, one can see to the right that there is a semicircular window. Standing immediately to the right of the entrance there is a stone calvary. The corbels on either side of the porch are busts of St. George (right) and St. Joan of Arc (left). The standing statue to the left of the porch is the centurion who watched at the foot of the cross.

Passing the simple buttressed wall, which is the chapel of St. Francis, added in October 1913, one reaches the west end of the church. When viewed from the steps of the surrounding flats this gives an impressive presence to the area, with its massive stone cross set into the upper part of the west wall. On either side there are small lancet windows as if to symbolise St. Mary and St. John standing at the foot of the cross. Above the cross and just under the eaves is the sanctus bell.

Following round the west end of the church one comes to

South porch and Calvary.

South porch – centurion.

South porch – Calvary.

South porch – St Joan.

South porch – St George.

St Francis chapel. Left: recent. Right: vintage.

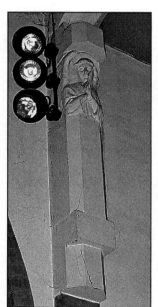

Angel corbel in St Francis chapel.

the north-west entrance, which is a pair of double doors under a simple lintel. Surrounding this porch is an array of six niches for statues, which unfortunately have never been added. At the east end of the north wall one finds that the church adjoins the old mission church.

The plain severity of the exterior does not prepare one for the array of shrines and decorations that beautify the stark plainness of the interior as one enters by the south entrance. This church is a tall, simple, brick building with six bays of capital-less brick arcades, arch braced roof, passage aisles, an additional chapel on the south side and an apsidal chancel with a narrow ambulatory.

Goodhart-Rendel had decided opinions about this church. He found a "sinister artiness" about it with its odd internal use of Fletton bricks. He said that "everything seems to be deliberately

East end.

West end.

unmeaning and odd". But there is no need to agree with him!

The interior appears lofty and spacious and because of the large clerestory windows (mainly with plain glass) is very light. The two eastern-most nave bays have deep clerestory recesses that form the false transepts. On either side of the nave there are narrow passage aisles. The bays formed by the nave arcades are set aside for devotional shrines. The nave and chancel are separated by a low brick wall with a short return topped with a stone coping. The chancel arch is formed from two Gothic arches, one superimposed over the other. The apse roof is supported by a half cartwheel like construction. The chancel is narrower than the nave and terminates in a polygonal apse pierced by five tall lancet windows. It is encircled by an ambulatory passage that is pierced by seven Gothic shaped openings. The chancel is raised three steps above the nave with a further step dividing it from the sanctuary area. The high altar is then raised a further three steps, in accordance with Catholic worship for which St. Silas was designed.

The high altar is therefore seven steps above the level of the nave and to heighten one's focus, Shearman designed the great baldacchino (or ciborium) to rise above the altar. It is here that Shearman embodies the concept of the Baroque idea of the dramatic altar, that from the moment the worshippers enter the church they should see the altar and be drawn towards it and that from the magnificence of its decoration, they should be reminded of the glory and wonder of the eucharist.

The baldacchino is undoubtedly Shearman's finest interior fitting in any of his churches and was a gift by Alice Mary Hunt in 1914. She had attended the consecration and was so impressed by the church at that time, she promised £50, but then sent a cheque for £500. The baldacchino has at the centre of the pediment the Resurrection figure of Our Lord with the banner of victory in His hand and surrounded by an aureole. Below is the word "Resurrexit". To the sides of Christ are two angels holding censers and two more attendant figures bearing incense boats. On the pillars at each corner are angels blowing trumpets. Above the figure of Our Lord is a dove, representing the Holy Spirit. Above are the letters in flames of red and gold D.O.M. (Deo Optimo Maximo) or "To the Most High God". This is emblematic of the encircling radiance of the Divine Glory and is based on the account of the Transfiguration.

Follow the ambulatory passage to the right of the chancel and one reaches the lady chapel which faces south-east with its cleverly handled construction of the vaulting that changes direction as the chapel opens up. Similarly, if one follows the ambulatory passage to the left side of the chancel one can enter the quiet and beautiful chapel dedicated to St. Thomas of Canterbury. Over the altar is a fine reredos and canopy painted by Henry Victor Milner in 1918. It shows in the

North arcade.

South arcade.

South arcade.   **Clerestory windows.**

centre the Virgin worshipping the infant Christ. Above is the text "Et Verbum caro factum est"- "and the Word was made flesh". On either side are the Archangel Gabriel and the Virgin Mary and below are the words of the annunciation "Ave Maria gratia plena Dominus tecum benedicta tu in mulieribus"- "Hail Mary full of grace, the Lord is with thee, blessed art thou among women". Across the top of the reredos is a reference to the use of the chapel for the Reservation of the Blessed Sacrament, "Adoremus in Aeternum Sanctissimum Sacramentum" – "Let us adore for ever the most Holy Sacrament".

There is a west organ loft and choir gallery. Above this gallery is a small stained glass window depicting St. Cecilia, in memory of Georgiana Sophia Whittingham. Below the figure are the words "Veni Accipe Coronam" – "Come receive your crown" set to plainsong. St. Cecilia is playing a hand held organ at which sits an angel. Two further angels look down on her. This window was executed by Henry Victor Milner, a well known stained-glass artist who lived in Camden. In the lower half of the window can be found the rare monogram of Milner. Below the gallery is the very plain brick and stone font which was probably the only one designed by Shearman and although stark is very much in keeping with the rest of his vision for the church..

On the south side of the west wall above the gallery is a stained glass window of the Madonna and Child, beneath which is a small

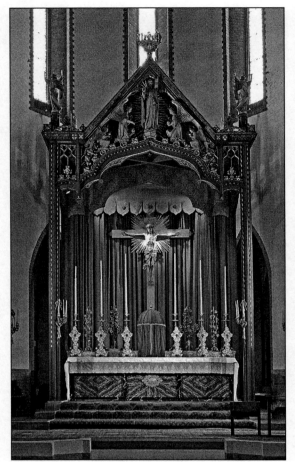

Sanctuary with baldacchino (left) and unadorned baldacchino (right).

panel depicting the Annunciation. The subject of the Madonna in this window was taken from a painting by Botticelli. This window is also from the workshop of Henry Victor Milner.

From the organ loft there is access to a second floor chapel, now no longer in use due to its inaccessibility, but originally dedicated to St. George. It was placed facing east and much used in the early history of the church. It gives a stunning view into the church and a feeling of standing on the edge of a cliff. Within this chapel there is a stained glass window, also by Milner, generally unnoticed from the body of the church, of St. Michael the Archangel with a naked kneeling figure being weighed in a balance against a green dragon. Above the figure of St. Michael are a trumpeting angel and an entwined scroll with the words "We praise thee O God". This window was a gift from the artist himself, who was a member of the congregation.

Each of the bays in the nave has now been set aside for a particular devotional purpose. The south chapel, which is dedicated to St. Francis of Assisi but is now the sacristy, is complete with its own altar and tabernacle. It was originally designed by Shearman in

High Altar crucifix and candlestick designed by ECS.

October 1913. When the chapel was adapted in 1990 to become the sacristy the arches were filled in between the south passage aisle and the chapel itself. The chapel comprises four high bays with Soanian vaulting and piers on which stylised angels are carved. The windows were presented and designed by Milner in 1915. One depicts San Francesco (St. Francis of Assisi) holding an open book and in the panel below there is a shield containing a crucifix surrounded by angel wings. The other window depicts Santa Chiara (St. Clare) holding an open book and a crozier and in the panel below there is a shield showing a chalice and host surrounded by an aureole. In the roof of the sacristy are glazed oculi.

In the south wall above the sacristy is a stained glass window of a slightly later date than those

Apse roof.

by Milner. This window by Louis Davis dates from 1922, from a design of 1907 and depicts "Spes" – "Hope", with the title "Laus Deo". It is in the style of the Arts and Crafts Movement and shows Hope tip-toeing through daffodils and looking heavenward.

Little provision was made in the original church for the clergy. A room for the priest was provided up a narrow winding staircase to the left of the apse and behind St. Thomas' Chapel. The sacristy was under the former mission church, accessible from a door in the ambulatory.

Sanctuary arches.

Ambulatory passage.

Lady chapel.

Devotionally St. Silas is probably the most complete of the five North London churches and is designed for the enactment of the Mass in true Catholic fashion.

The whole church is resplendent with statues of the Saints. Two major statues depicting St. Silas and St. Paul were designed by Benjamin Consitt Boulter, who was a prominent member of the congregation. A fine set of painted stations of the cross adorn the west side of the columns. These were made by Sister Dorina of the Sisters of the Church at Kilburn. They were originally a dark sepia colour but were painted by Nina Somerset who also designed banners which hang on the columns facing into the nave. Relics of many Saints are to be found both on the high altar and the minor altars and these are

Lady chapel.

Lady chapel roof.   **Lady chapel.**

evidence of the profound level of Catholic worship which takes place
here.

The six large candlesticks behind the high altar were designed by
Shearman. They were originally bronze but were later silver-plated. The
crucifix from the set now stands in the confessional area adjacent to
the sacristy. The silver lamp hanging on the south side of the
sanctuary was also designed by Shearman and is in a striking art
nouveau style.

The Parish records suggest that Shearman was very fond of St.
Silas Church and may well have worshipped here. His name appears
occasionally over a number of years in the list of those who gave money
to the church for flowers. Other sources suggest that he was a high
churchman and would have been very much at home here. The total
concept of St. Silas and his other churches, indicate a thorough
knowledge of Anglo-Catholic ritual and worship.

Priests-in-Charge of St. Silas:-

1912	George Napier Whittingham
1930	Frank Lacy Hillier
1963	Douglas Arthur Cobb
1987	Philip Dyson
1989	Graeme Charles Rowlands

St Thomas chapel.

Font.

St Thomas chapel.

St Thomas chapel.

APPENDIX

Letters from Shearman to the Incorporated Church Building Society with reference to St. Silas.

Byrnelmscote,
Winchester.
29 Nov 1911

Dear Sir,

St. Silas Kentish Town

Thank you for your letter of the 25th inst.

I am sending you herewith the drawings etc. of this new church for submission to your Committee of Architects & trust you will obtain for us such approval as may enable us to begin without prejudice to the obtaining of a grant from the Society. Valuable time has been lost.

Chancery proceedings – a disputed will, under which S. Silas was to benefit, with some other institutions who tried to take all except £50 – has cost the church a good deal of what it was intended to have and I have to do a lot for the money. A plain church, simple, dignified – stately I trust – is my endeavour, with no money spent on what is merely ornament.

I enclose a few notes on the structure & shall be happy to give any further information you may desire.

Yrs. very faithfully

Ernest C. Shearman

Byrnelmscote,
Winchester.
12 December 1911

Dear Sir,

New Church of S. Silas
Kentish Town

I return the drawings & specification of this church, and in acknowledging the response of the Committee of Honorary Architects will ask you to be so kind as to lay my reply before them.

Concrete foundations under piers and aisle walls. I think the Committee hardly do justice to the thick bed of cement concrete – reinforced – over the whole site, and the continuous deep masses of similar concrete under piers and walls, all one solid mass.

To add to this would I submit, call for an addition to the cost of

84

the church which is not needed. The foundation is extremely strong, and I have to be very careful with money.

The opinion of your strong Committee however weighs much with me, and I have today seen the District Surveyor who has an extended experience of this particular soil, with the result that I have added an extra breadth of concrete to the inner trench and increased the reinforced bed between the trenches to 2 feet 0 inches and with this, back by a happy experience of this foundation on a worse site, I trust I may gain the approval of your Committee.

<u>Thickness of buttresses</u>. Here again I must plead rigid economy – and a satisfactory personal experience. I was in a church built on these lines – foundations included, please – only yesterday where I am adding the groined ceiling to the sanctuary.

This church was approved by your Committee in both these particulars and had to thank you for a substantial grant.

There has not been any settlement and in spite of an added width of span of 3 feet 0 inches not a single joint of the similar roof has opened. Everything is perfect – viewed from the sanctuary scaffolding.

That in replying to your Committee on the buttress question I would rest trust solely to my own experience.

In most churches of my acquaintance, the buttresses are less in width than the piers and in this development of Gothic vaulting the tendency was to deep comparatively thin buttresses.

In dealing with Winchester Cathedral, where the need for great care and thought is very obvious, Mr. Jackson's new buttresses are less than 3 feet 0 inches thick – not a quarter the width of piers.

I do not find that my own buttresses look mean or "skinny" & they certainly do their work well with their depth of resistance – some 10 feet over all.

May I hope your committee will accept this defence.

<u>Flats.</u> These are of asphalt, not of lead, but the small lead gutter will be 8 lbs lead, not 6 lbs lead – an error in specification.

<u>Rise in floor to west</u> – The floor level will be flat. I am very glad but beg to thank your Committee for their opinion.

<u>Other windows – more light.</u> I will gladly follow your Committee's wishes in this matter, but will ask them to bear in mind that I was asked for a "dark Church". Many Churches in very poor districts are not well lighted – St. Alban Holborn, St. Mary Magdalene's, Munster Square for example: a strong light shows up poor clothes rather mercilessly.

Our neighbours on the south west object to windows overlooking their property – and windows in Preston Street will lead to trouble.

I am ready to add glass domes in the concrete roofs of the aisles, if that will meet your Committees wishes.

Lastly. Your Committee ask for 3 feet 0 inch back to back seats. I beg them to consider that the Ecclesiastical Commissioners accept 2 feet 10½ inches – and has done so in this case: that if I reduce the accommodation I shall not satisfy the Bishops' Fund Committee who require so much accommodation – that the site is limited & was costly. I must make the most of it. I always put 3 feet 0 inch, when I can, but with good chairs, 2 feet 10½ inches allows enough for devout kneeling and more than enough for quiet rest & spiritual instruction, and a great deal of that is required in the parts around Preston Street.

I trust I shall gain your Committee's approval by these explanations. We want to begin at once, but we want to have the help that your Society can give us.

In pleading economy, I do not think that I ask you to approve anything mean, or unworthy the great aims of your Society & its Committee of Honorary Architects.

>   I beg to remain
>   Yours very faithfully
>   Ernest C. Shearman

>   Winchester 18 December 1912

Gentlemen,

>   S. Silas New Church
>   Kentish Town.

I beg to certify that this Church has been consecrated and in use for a number of weeks.

The recommendations of your Committee of Honorary Architects were duly carried out: eight extra windows being inserted in north and south clerestory, one extra at the west end (a valuable addition of afternoon sun) and two small windows in north aisle. Even on a dull day, there is abundance of light.

Messrs James Burges & Sons Builders of Wycliffe Road, Wimbledon. S.W. have carried out their contract with the ability & thoroughness which always bring credit to this field & satisfaction to their employees.

>   I am
>   Gentlemen
>   Yours very faithfully

>   Ernest C. Shearman

ST. BARNABAS, NORTH EALING

The history of St. Barnabas starts in 1905 when money was given to buy a plot of land to build a temporary corrugated iron mission church at the junction of Castlebar Park Road and Pitshanger Lane. This church was erected in 1907 and dedicated on 9th November of that year, but was soon outgrown by the population. It was planned to build a permanent church on the same site but this was not permitted. In December 1911 the present site, at the junction of Pitshanger Lane and Denison Road, was acquired and on 5th March 1913 it was finally announced that a new church would be built there. The Revd. Walter Mitchell was appointed to be the "Missioner" and to set up the building fund, as there was no parish at that time.

Ernest Shearman was appointed as architect, assisted by Ernest A. Tyler of Ealing. The designs were put out to tender and the estimate of £14,630 submitted by James Burges and Sons of Wimbledon, who were the builders both of St. Matthew's, Wimbledon (which was destroyed during the Second World War) and of St. Silas, Kentish Town, was accepted. The Ecclesiastical Commission

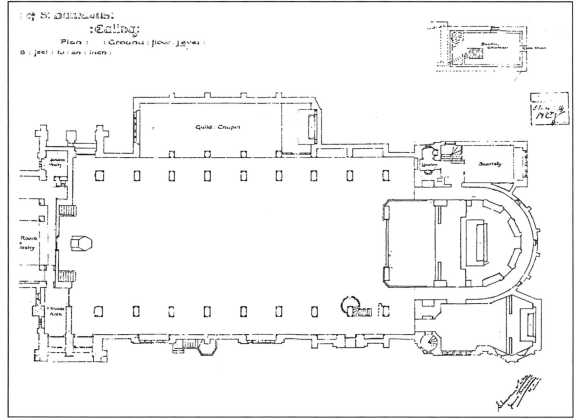

Architect's ground plan.

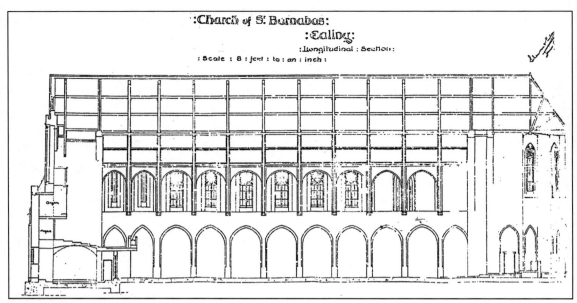

Architect's longitudinal section.

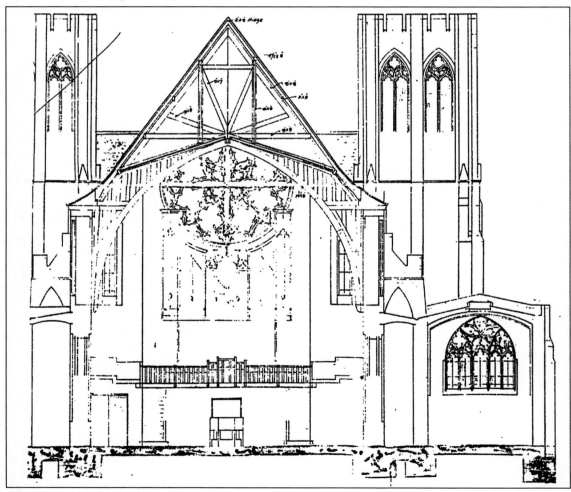

Architect's transverse section.

(equivalent to the Church Commissioners) insisted that this cost should be cut to £10,000. Shearman was asked to make a number of economies in the building work and the planned pair of west towers, the choir vestry, the upper sacristy and a bay in the nave were sacrificed. However he refused to compromise and remove the west rose window and wrote to that effect on 7th May 1914. This was accepted on 25th May 1914.

Funds for the church were raised from three main sources by the building committee. These were the Bishop of London's Fund for new churches, the Ecclesiastical Commission and the parish. Donations were forthcoming and the targets reached before the consecration of the church.

In March 1914 Shearman wrote that the "special wants [of the church] needed a lot of thinking out". Shortly afterwards James Burges & Sons of Wimbledon were appointed as builders.

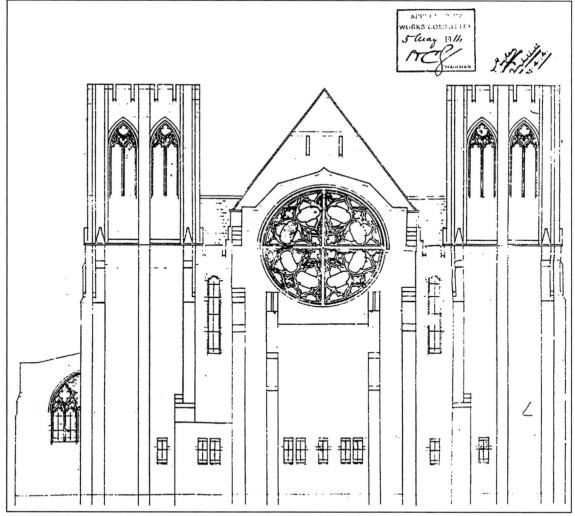

Architect's west elevation.

Laying foundation stone.

Foundation stone.

Vintage photograph of exterior.

On 13th June 1914 the foundation stone was laid by Mrs. Mary Baron and blessed by the Bishop of Kensington, the Rt. Revd. John Primatt Maud. The stone is to be found at the base of the south pier carrying the chancel arch. The foundation stone has not been inscribed and this would conform to Shearman's idea that such a stone should not be inscribed before it was laid.

After about a year there was a dispute over the poor quality of some of the timber, which needed to be replaced. This had been the subject of correspondence with the Ecclesiastical Commissioners even before work commenced. An anonymous note was sent listing six complaints about Shearman's professional conduct. Furthermore, he had neglected to tell the builders that the towers were not being built and

Vintage photograph of interior.

Apse and south elevation.

South elevation.

consequently the builders had hoisted 15,000 bricks unnecessarily on to the roof. These problems resulted in Burges threatening to withdraw from the work before it was finished. The building committee decided as a result of this to dismiss Shearman, which was done by letter dated 8th June 1915 and to appoint Tyler as sole architect, which was done by letter a week later.

The church was consecrated on 3rd June 1916 by the Bishop of London, the Rt. Revd. Arthur Foley Winnington-Ingram.

In February 1917 Passmore inspected the church

West elevation and porch.

on behalf of the Ecclesiastical Committee and various minor faults were put right. Burges, who in June 1916 had requested an arbitration with regard to the dispute over the timber and brickwork, found favour with Passmore and was vindicated. After a hearing on 26th April 1917 Burges was awarded his costs and praised for his loyalty and steady work in completing the church.

The parish officially came into being through an Order in Council on 10th August 1917 and the Revd. Walter Mitchell was inducted as vicar on 3rd November 1917.

However, this was not the last that was seen of Shearman because in 1927 the stone figure of St. Barnabas was completed for the south porch and was dedicated by the Bishop of Kensington in June of that year. In 1935 he was consulted for the building of the upper room above the sacristy, for which an anonymous donation of £400 was given and yet again in April 1936 he made plans for a Parish Hall costing about £5,000.

This was the first of the three West London churches to express Shearman's characteristic Mediterranean Gothic style, which he had already tried at St. Matthew's, Wimbledon and St. Silas, Kentish Town, North London.

Here there is dramatic flowing window tracery offset by austere dark purple brick walls with stone bands. The spacious interior has a broad arch-braced roof, passage aisles behind plain painted brick arches and capital-less pillars. The apse roof is supported by a half cartwheel shaped framework, as in St. Silas and St. Gabriel. The width of the nave embraces both the chancel and the narrow ambulatory around the apse. There are nine bays in the nave in total. The first is narrow as are the last two which hide under the gallery. There are five pairs of tall lancet clerestory windows in the apse. Also between the chancel and the ambulatory are five simple lancet shaped openings. The west end has a large rose window with cruciform mullion and transom. The west gallery houses the organ and seating for the choir. In the south passage aisle are two five-light windows.

A most unusual feature is the small south lady chapel with its own tiny gallery and stunningly leaded east rose window with flowing tracery. In its south wall is a five-light window of similar design to those in the nave. Regrettably, in 1993, the arch above the gallery in

Porch.

Statue of St Barnabas above porch.

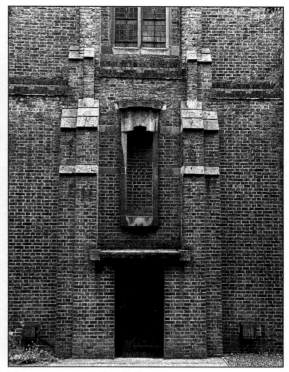

Doorway and niche.

Turret staircase.

the west wall of this chapel was bricked up. Previously it was possible, when viewing the gallery from the east end of the chapel, to have sight of a stone stairway apparently leading heavenward, but in reality giving access to the south false transept. The gallery space can still be reached by a spiral stone stairway through a doorway just outside the glass doors to this chapel. A glass screen was added between the south side of the chancel and the lady chapel and a further arch from the nave was also bricked up. However, this chapel has been beautified by a triptych painted by Sister Theresa Margaret, a hermit with the Community of the Holy Name, Pwllheli, North Wales and added in June 1996 in time for the Church's 80th Anniversary.

South chapel.

Original plans included a north nave chapel, but this was never built. There was also to be a parish room below the west gallery flanked by a west tower.

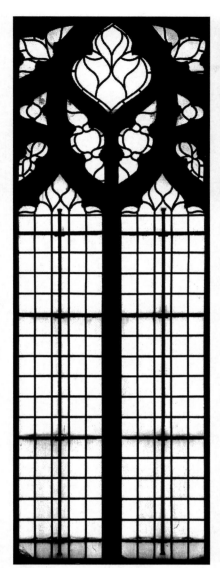

Clerestory windows.

In 1936 the upper room designed by Shearman was built above the sacristy on the north side of the chancel. This room has a small, round tripartite window of typical Shearman origin with swirling glass shapes of a similar design to that previously used at St. Francis of Assisi, Isleworth.

At the south-west corner are paired entrance arches with flattened ogee heads. These arches were to be surmounted by a tower which is unfinished. A second tower was also planned at the north-west corner of the church. Within the arch of the south-west entrance there is a statue representing St. Barnabas, designed by Shearman, which was added as a memorial to the first vicar, the Revd. Walter Mitchell, who died in 1926.

Probably the most stunning feature of St. Barnabas is the magnificent mural in the sanctuary. It was painted in 1917 by James Clark (1857-1943) and portrays a host of Angels and Saints worshipping the Risen Lord, symbolised at its centre by a Dove and a chalice and host. Clark describes the subject of his mural as *Three Hierarchies of Angels praising and adoring the Holy Trinity*. In the centre panel are Symbols of the Father, Son and Holy Spirit. The upper choir has Cherubim, Seraphim, Thrones and Archangels Uriel and

East end.

West end.

South arcade.

South chapel.

Raphael. The central choir has Kings, Judges and Warriors. The lower choir has Princes, Messengers and Musicians. Measurements of the whole work are:– length 69ft, height 25ft. Under the mural are the words *Therefore with Angels and Archangels and with all the Company of Heaven we Laud and Magnify thy Glorious Name evermore praising Thee and Praying Holy Holy Holy.* Some members of the first congregation of St. Barnabas acted as models for the painting. The two archangels guarding the chancel are also by James Clark and were painted on to the walls in 1925 as a memorial to Mrs. Mitchell, the vicar's wife.

There are five two-light lancet windows in the apse given in 1916 by Stanley and Rosa Burgess. In the upper parts of these windows are the following from left to right: St. Matthew, St. John, The Paschal Lamb, St. Mark and St. Luke. Below them are found the following figures: St. Andrew and St. George, St. Peter and St. James the Great, Christ Condemned and Christ the King, St. Barnabas and St. Paul, St. Patrick and St. David. Beneath these are smaller pictures generally depicting various events: St. Columba in Iona, St. Augustine preaching in Kent, Lord not my feet only, Thy will be done, Christ rejected by this world, Christ rules in the Kingdom in Heaven, Touch me not, Feed my sheep, St. Bridget preaching in Ireland and the Alleluia victory.

There is also one lower window in the apse and this is seen immediately behind the high altar showing Christ holding a sheaf of corn. The wording on this window is *Bread of Life* and the picture in the lower part of the window is of the supper at Emmaus.

There are two five-light stained glass windows in the south aisle, which were installed in 1922. That on the left portrays the Nativity with

James Clark's mural in sanctuary.

South chapel looking west.

Apse with sacristy and upper room.

Saints and elders, while the other portrays Archangel Michael at the centre, flanked by David, Jonathan, Gideon and Joshua. Above them are the Royal Coats of Arms and the shields of England, Scotland and France. All the windows in the church are by Clayton & Bell.

The large floor-mounted crucifix standing in its base of fossil marble in the north passage aisle, the altar to the Sacred Heart, the stations of the cross (designed by the Community of the Sisters of the Church, originally based in Kilburn) and statue to the Blessed Virgin Mary are all witness to the Anglo-Catholic ambience of this church.

The organ came from the church of All Hallows, St. Pancras in 1916 and cost £300.

The banner of St. Barnabas was embroidered in about 1916.

The church has the following pictures:

South chapel window.

Nave window.

South chapel window. **Shrine in north passage aisle.**

North-east aisle – *Holy Trinity 1516-1550* by Pedro
      Machuca with alterations by Antonio Bazzi *(Sodoma)*
South aisle – *The Nativity,* painter unknown
South aisle – *The Guardian Angel,* copy of painting by
      Guercino (1591-1666)
Vicars of St. Barnabas:

1917 – 1926	Walter Mitchell
1926 – 1951	H. Salter Barrett
1951 – 1976	Richard Nevill Hetherington
1977 – 1988	Ronald Frederick Swan
1990 – 1999	Gerald Alfred Reddington
2000 – 2005	Neil Nicholls
2006 – 2007	Carl le Prevost
2007:	David Deboys

Station of the Cross.

Organ loft.

Font and east end.

Pulpit.

Pulpit.

Apse and sanctuary roof.

ST. GABRIEL, ACTON

St. Gabriel is chronologically the third of Shearman's North London churches, but externally most resembles St. Matthew, Wimbledon, which was destroyed during the Second World War. It was built by Dove Brothers, Islington, mainly of brick with stone facings and string courses. Work on the church was started on 28th October 1929 and the Rt. Hon. Sir Montague Barlow laid the foundation stone on 8th November 1930. As is customary in Shearman churches, the foundation stone is at the base of the chancel arch on the south side at the entrance to the lady chapel. Like all the other churches it does not have a tower. In common with the others it has an apse, but with seven single lancet windows in the sanctuary and chancel area. It does not have an ambulatory passage, but there are five gothic shaped recesses and two openings in the apse. There are two steps from the nave to the chancel and an additional two steps between the chancel and sanctuary, where it retains its altar rail.

The high altar is further raised on three steps, which surround it on three sides. Choir stalls are placed in the chancel. On the south side there are two openings into the lady chapel. The apse has a half cartwheel shaped roof brace, as is also found in St. Silas and St. Barnabas, Pitshanger Lane.

Laying foundation stone.

The lady chapel is adjacent to the chancel and is approached from the east end of the south passage aisle. There are a total of four Gothic arches into this chapel: one from the passage aisle; one from the south-east corner of the nave; a large arch with two steps into the chancel and a narrow arch with three steps from the north side of the lady chapel altar to the side of the high altar. On the step from the lady chapel nave to its chancel there is an altar rail. The lady chapel altar is itself elevated on a further step, which surrounds it on three sides. Just to the west of the altar rail there is a Soanian arch, which helps to divide the chapel visually. This chapel is well lit by a pair of two-light windows in the south wall. The Blessed Sacrament is reserved here.

There are passage aisles extending along the length of the nave, each having six bays of three differing sizes. From east to west the first arch is the narrowest, the second a little wider and the third to sixth are the widest.

However, the church is still incomplete. This can be most easily seen from the exterior, which still shows the west wall filled by temporary brickwork. Original drawings exist for a rose window at the west end of the nave. From the inside of the church, it can be seen that further economies had to be made. This seems to have included limiting the number of clerestory windows, as there are recesses where they should have been. On the north side there is a single lancet window serving the false transept. There are no clerestory windows above the third and fifth bays on the north side or the fourth or sixth bays on the south side. However, there is a rose window, which can only be seen in its entirety from outside the church. It is situated in the south transept and can best be seen from the road. It is a four-petal rose with broad cruciform transom and mullion. From inside the church a little over half of this window can be seen at any one time. The clerestory windows in the nave contain two-lights and there is also a four-light window in the fourth bay in the south wall of the nave.

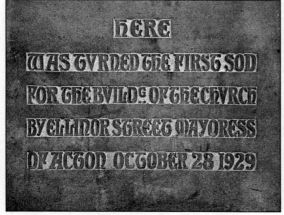

Turning of the first sod: 1929.

Foundation stone: 1930.

Apse and south elevation.

Incomplete west end and south elevation.

Chancel and Nave 1931-1932.

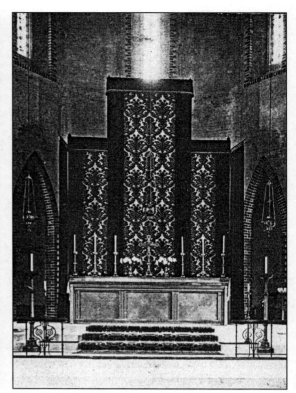

High Altar 1931-1932.

The vestry is situated in the northeast corner of the church and is entered through an arch at the east end of the north passage aisle. To the south of this entrance is a deep recess, which is in the position where an arch to the north side of the ambulatory would have been.

The west end of the church is cut off by a brick narthex with windows and central doors. Above this is the gallery, although the organ is not housed here. The south wall of the gallery has a two-light clerestory window but the north wall does not, although there is an arched recess. The entrance to the church is through the double doors at the southwest corner under the vestigial tower into the narthex. There is also a

East end.

East end.

Sanctuary.

111

smaller door in the south wall under the false transept and into the most easterly bay.

The nave columns bear a remarkable similarity to all the other Shearman churches, even to the number of brick courses. In common with St. Silas it has a stepped brick and stone-capped wall between the chancel and the nave, but of its own design.

St. Gabriel is without some of the finer fittings of the two earlier churches, but it does however have its own treasures. Unique items are the two fine low-relief terracotta panels by George Tinworth, which are placed on either side of the chancel arch and were given to the church in 1930. The one on the north side shows Moses and the serpent while that on the south shows Christ being taken down from the Cross. Edward VII originally commissioned them for his wife Alexandra. They were exhibited in the Paris Exhibition of 1878 and were formerly in Sandringham Church, Norfolk. In 1861 George Tinworth (1843 – 1913) studied at the School of Art, Lambeth under John Sparke and in 1864 at the Royal Academy School. He joined the firm of Doulton's in 1867 and remained with them until his death. His output was devoted almost entirely to religious subjects. This church is truly fortunate to have two of his works.

There is a rumour that the font may have originated from Westminster Abbey and that the glass of the apse clerestory windows may have originated from a church in Portman Square.

Shearman's design here was for Anglo-Catholic worship. There are sepia coloured stations of the cross, whose origin is the same as those of St. Silas and St. Barnabas, Pitshanger Lane, which is the Community of the Sisters of the Church. He allowed for the altar to be placed in an elevated position and the three sanctuary lamps indicate the type of worship to be found here.

This church has currently been reordered so that it has a nave altar with seating facing in three directions, not as Shearman intended. Shearman designed his churches for Tractarian worship with an altar elevated to eye level.

Vicars of St. Gabriel:

1913	W. Marsh Rapson (Missioner)
1928	C.V. Camplin Cogan
1946	E. Aykroyd Jones
1953	S.E. Adams
1962	Brian William Horlock
1968	John Robert Patrick Ashby
1981	Edwin James Alcock
2002	Keith Adrian Robus

APPENDIX

Copy of letter from Ernest C. Shearman to the Secretary of the Incorporated Church Building Society.

London.
3rd May 1927.

Dear Sir,

St. Gabriel's New Church, Acton.
I have to thank you for the report of your Committee of Architects.
The north wall of the north chapel, the first portion to be built, is only 1 foot 6 inches thick. Money is very short, but I think it should be a little stronger.
Instead of adding 4½ inches to its thickness, I should be glad to add piers on the inside, opposite the aisle piers, & so carry down the lines of the vault ribs. I show this treatment in pencil on the plan of the complete Church.
Will this commend itself to your Committee of Architects?
As regards the asphalt roof, I shall be glad to adopt their suggestion.
The floor covering will probably be of wood block, as soon as money to pay for it is available.
For the same reason (no money) the means of heating must be limited, for the present, to gas or oil stoves.
With thanks to Members of the Committee & to yourselves.

Believe me to be
Yours very faithfully,
Ernest C Shearman

I would add that the cost of piers to the north wall would be less than the cost of thickening the whole wall & would stiffen it even more. At the same time, extra elbow room would be given.
Further, the introduction of piers would reduce to some order the varied collection of pictures which churches seem to attract.

E.C.S.

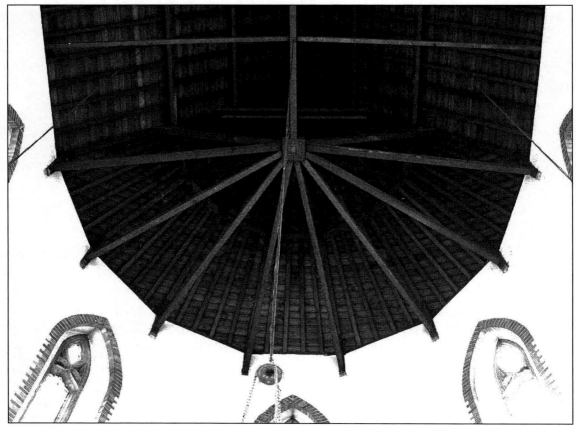

Sanctuary roof.

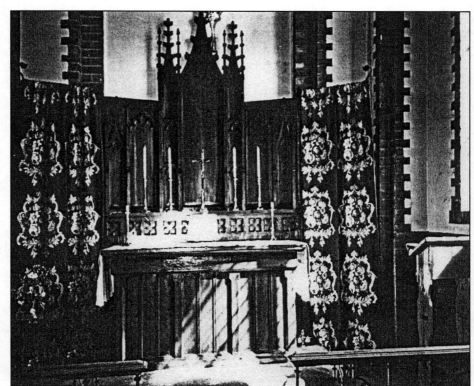

Vintage photograph of the lady chapel reredos.

Shrine of Our Lady of Walsingham using the Lady chapel reredos.

Lady chapel with painting of the annunciation.

Lady chapel.

Passage aisle.

Architect's drawing of west elevation and proposed rose window.

Windowless north bays.

Window south nave.

Window south nave.

Window south nave.

Window south nave.

Windows west elevation.

Window south nave.

Apse lancet window.

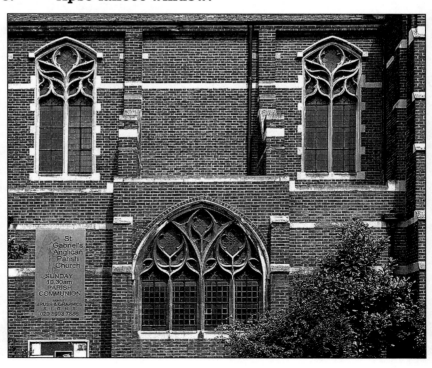

Windows south nave.

Clerestory windows south nave.

North arcade.

South arcade.

West end.

Font.

South chapel altar rail.

**George Tinworth relief of
Moses and the serpent.**

**George Tinworth relief
of the Deposition of
Christ from the cross.**

Station of the Cross.

Pulpit.

Pulpit.

Lectern.

123

Original chandelier.

ST. BARNABAS, TEMPLE FORTUNE

his church is sadly no longer in Anglican use. It was built on an island site and is orientated almost north to south. Therefore any description of direction refers to the liturgical direction, e.g. the high altar would be at the east end of the church.

Shearman's church was built to replace a very modest parish hall, which had been built in 1915, dedicated as a temporary church and consecrated in 1923. In April 1931 Shearman was appointed to draw up plans to build a new church on the axis of the former church. By June 1931 he had already submitted plans of a church which included a tower. Various delays occurred, but the foundation stone was eventually laid in June 1932. Shearman had strong views about foundation stones which have already been set out.

During 1932-1934 the east end of the church was built. This included the apse and sanctuary, the vicar's vestry, the choir vestry, the lady chapel and the first two bays of the nave. At this point the building work had reached the eastern wall of the old church. Further delays occurred and Shearman died in April 1939 before the church

Architect's drawing of exterior.

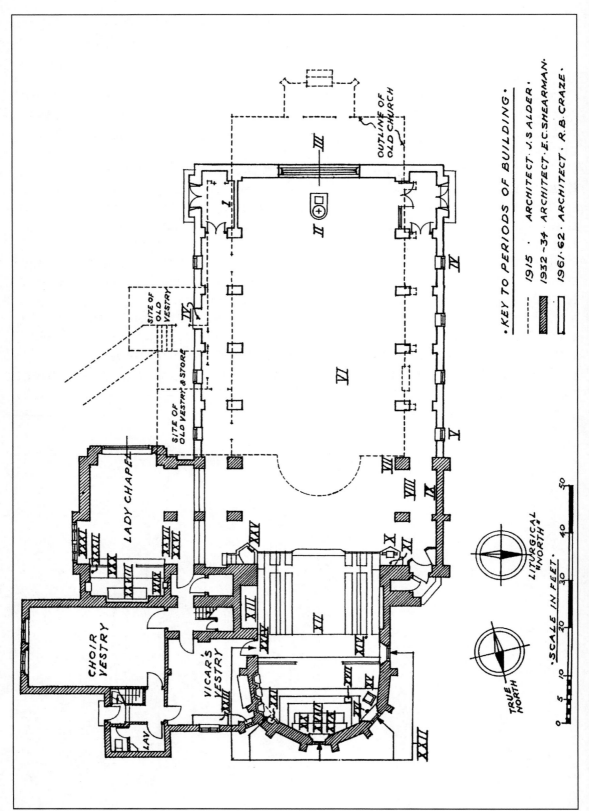

Architect's ground plan.

was completed. However, he had been able to complete the plans for the remaining nave bays and the west end of the church.

In September 1940 two bombs hit the church: one penetrated the outer roof of the chancel and the other landed on the flat roof of what was hoped one day would become the tower. In 1945 the church was repaired.

The church was finally completed in 1962 under the care of the distinguished ecclesiastical architect Romilly B. Craze, very much to the original plans. The foundation stone of the 1915 church was incorporated into the north wall of the nave.

The Bishop of Edmonton, the Rt. Revd. Brian Masters presided at the closure of the church on Saturday, 1st October 1994 at a sung eucharist.

Since 1996 the building has been used by the Coptic Church and has been adapted to their form of worship. Much of the chancel is now obscured by the iconostasis. Additional building work has also been done but in a style compatible with the original structure. A new entrance with three doors and eight small rectangular windows above has been created at the west end, the style of which is totally in accordance with the windows at the north west of the church. A robing

Foundation stone of 1915 church.

Apse and north elevation.

West and north elevation.

room has also been added at the north east end of the church adjacent to the chancel area.

The chancel has a vaulted roof; round its periphery are shields bearing the symbols of saints, which from left to right are St. Alban, St. Paul, St. James the Great, Ecce Agnus Dei, St. Andrew, St. George, St. Patrick, the Blessed Virgin Mary, St. John, St. Peter, St. Louis of Toulouse and St. Barnabas, who since he has no symbol is represented by the letter B. Along the central line of the vaulting are the symbols of the Trinity, the Chalice and the Son of Righteousness; grouped around the latter are the symbols and instruments of the Passion of Christ, which from left to right are the money bag of Judas, the scourging pillar and rope, the scourges, the crown of thorns, the three crosses of Calvary, the hammer, nails and pincers, the dice box and dice, the reed and sponge, the spear with vase of spices, and the ladder.

St. Barnabas contains a large number of Shearman's internal fittings. These fittings include items such as pulpit with tester, lectern, altar rail, the Bishop's chair, sedilia seats, choir stalls, organ loft panelling, a carved stand for flowers and possibly the nave seating.

There is an apse with five single lancet windows, but no ambulatory. The roof of the sanctuary and chancel is atypical of Shearman in that it is vaulted with ribs. There are the typical narrow

West elevation.

passage aisles, but with no signs of previous stations of the cross, which are a feature of his other churches.

There are two rose windows. The one in the west wall of the lady chapel is typical of Shearman's ornamentation, but the one at the west end, completed so many years after his death, has only squared glass panels and is probably not as he intended. It appears from the original sketches submitted by Shearman to have been a very decorative six petal window similar to the design for the west window at St. Gabriel which was not completed.

The original sketch also shows an elaborate west double doorway

Apse and south chapel.

Chancel.

East end.

with a gothic shaped tympanum. Above the doorway would have been a
shallow gallery with battlements and three additional small gothic
windows behind it. The other notable feature of this sketch is the
south-east octagonal tower. This was also not built, but instead a
simple square tower was built to the north-east. The sketch of the nave
shows clerestory double lancet windows (probably four) and buttresses
between them, instead of the full height single lancets which were
substituted. There is a pair of additional four or five-light windows in
the north wall similar to those designed for the south wall of St.
Barnabas, Pitshanger Lane.

There is a small organ loft on the south side of the chancel. This
is reached by a stairway between the chancel and the choir vestry. The
stairway also leads to a room above the lady chapel. The chancel and
sanctuary floor is of Derbyshire fossil marble and is rather fine.

An Art Deco style aumbry in the lady chapel is set in a panel of
green marble. On the door of the aumbry are three vine leaves. A
bunch of grapes made from purple stones form the escutcheon for the
lock. The design is very similar to the aumbry in St. Francis of Assisi.

There is stained glass in the apse windows which depict Our
Blessed Lord, the Virgin Mary, St. John, St. Paul and St. Barnabas.
There is additional stained glass in some of the windows of the nave. A

small but beautiful window in the north aisle, designed by a pupil of Karl Parsons, depicting the Blessed Virgin Mary is also worth seeing.

The high altar has a reredos showing the Risen Christ. This altar, known as the Altar of Redemption, illustrates Our Lord as the Son of God and his work of redemption for us and for our salvation. At the time of his death Shearman was working on the altar design in collaboration with the Vicar of St. Bartholomew's Church, Hyde, Winchester, the Revd. W. R. Parr. The altar is marquetry work in both wood and mother-of-pearl. Along the upper border of the altar are the words "*HIS SERVANTS SHALL SERVE HIM AND THEY SHALL SEE HIS FACE*" and along the lower border are the words "*THE LEAVES OF THE TREE – THE HEALING OF THE NATIONS*". In the middle of the frontal is a mother-of-pearl tree of life with a double rainbow over it, also in mother-of-pearl. At the sides of the frontal are four identical ciphers containing the letters ABM for St. Barnabas, apostle and martyr.

R. B. Craze was responsible for the Portland stone font which has fishes round its base and the font cover which has a small figure of St. John the Baptist on the top.

The lady chapel, which is situated off the south aisle, has an impressive rose window in its east wall. There was an altar (1932) and reredos designed by John Hinds, displaying scenes from the Nativity in high relief carving. The centre panel of the reredos triptych have a carving in high relief of the Blessed Virgin Mary, but the doors of the triptych are plain. The reredos and altar from the lady chapel have now been taken to the church of St. Alban the Martyr, Golders Green and fitted very successfully into the north transept. The sedilia seats from the sanctuary have also been taken out and adapted for use in St. Albans. John Hinds had also been commissioned earlier to produce a reredos for St. Matthew, Wimbledon and this adds emphasis to the pattern of similarity which runs through the churches of Shearman.

High Altar.

133

Coptic church interior.

High Altar.

Window south nave.

South arcade.

Coptic church – sanctuary with original high altar.

Apse roof.

Chapel altar and reredos now in St Alban, Golders Green.

136

ST. FRANCIS OF ASSISI, ISLEWORTH

This is a proud church on the Great West Road, a short distance from the Chiswick flyover. Its lofty apse, which faces this major road, is an eye witness to the traffic thundering past. None of Shearman's other churches can claim such a public image. This church is orientated north to south, with the apse facing north. Tucked away on its east side is the attached vicarage and vestries and on the west side is the church hall, all designed by Shearman.

The site was originally acquired through the offices of the vicar of All Saints, Isleworth so that a church could be built to serve both the Northumberland estate and also those employed by the factories on the Great West Road. Money for the purchase of the site was raised from the Diocesan Fund and a gift of £1,250 from the Forty-Five Churches Fund. This enabled a start to be made on the construction of the church hall. A similar contribution from the Diocesan Fund and the Ecclesiastical Commissioners enabled the hall to be completed and a further grant from these bodies went towards the cost of the vicarage. A donation of £7,000 from the newly appointed vicar, the Revd. Frederick Howard Harding, in memory of his wife Mary Ann Harding,

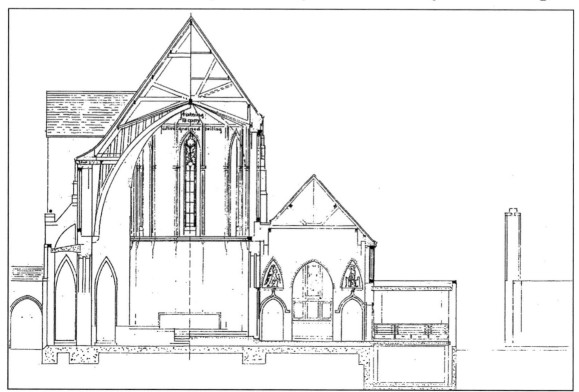

Architect's drawing of interior elevation looking east.

made possible an immediate start on the church building. The builders were again Dove Brothers, Islington. It is built of Claygate stock brick with contrasting stone bands externally with a slate roof and Fletton brick internally.

In the spring of 1934 the church hall was opened and services held there until the church itself was completed some 10 months later.

On 23rd March 1935 Bishop A.F. Winnington-Ingram of London consecrated the Church.

Some additional fittings were added in 1958 in memory of Father Harding, which included the Transfiguration Chapel with its altar, cross and candlesticks.

This is the last of Shearman's churches. Its apse has a high pitched roof and seven single lancet windows. There are also three string courses of stone encircling the apse. No provision was made for a spire or tower, although residual turrets could have been added to the capped-off mini towers at the junction of the chancel and nave, as was the case at S. Matthew, Wimbledon. Similar mini towers were also built at the ecclesiological west end of the church.

The sanctuary is set in a deep apse flanked by side chapels separated by paired lancet openings and reached by narrow passage aisles. These extend down the nave and are separated from the nave by a simple arcade making five bays. What appear as stunted transepts on

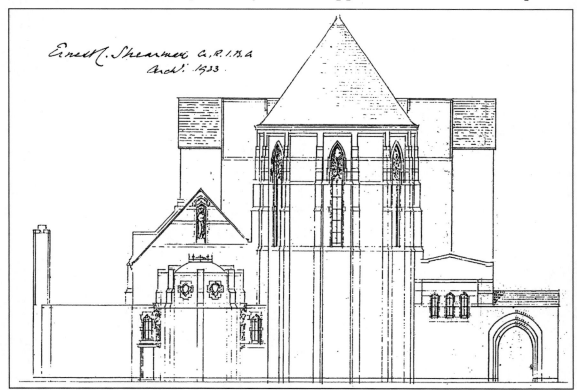

Architect's drawing of exterior elevation of apse and south chapel.

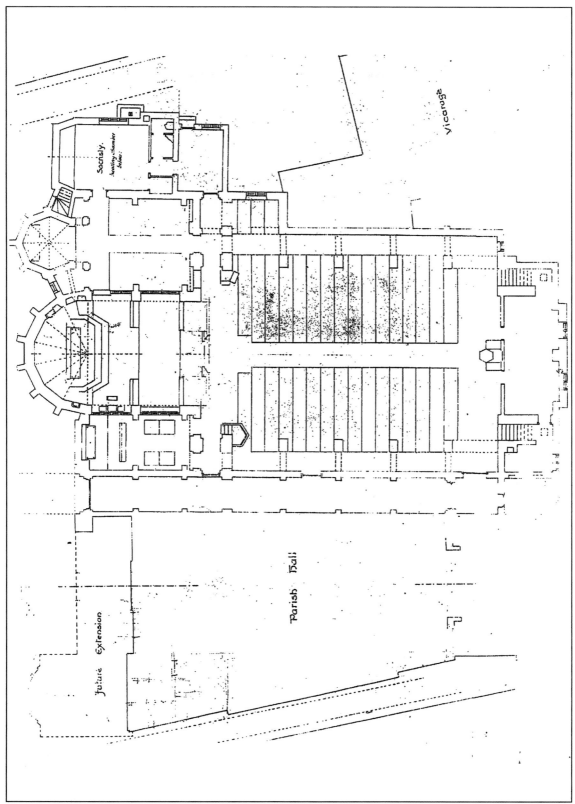

Architect's ground plan.

the exterior are contained within the passage aisles and side chapels internally. Stairs on either side of the west end lead to a small gallery housing the organ and seating for the choir. Viewed from the gallery this church has an uncanny architectural similarity to St. Silas, which was built twenty years earlier.

The impressive interior has great height and the usual passage aisles. The arcades have simple dying mouldings. The clerestory has two-light lancet windows in Early English style, which have reticulated tracery. The whole is pulled together by wooden transverse arches across the nave and their spandrels are filled with bold mullions. The chancel arch has to each side a Gothic arch which gives the impression of an ambulatory, but these in fact open into side chapels. The chancel ceiling is of painted acoustic panels. The nave has an open timber ceiling with arched trusses. The nave and chancel are divided from each other by a simple low brick wall which has a short return into the chancel and is capped with stone blocks.

The high altar is set up a total of seven steps with three steps surrounding it to allow for Catholic worship. There is no provision for choir to occupy the chancel, but a second simple altar has been placed on the third step partly obscuring the magnificent carved high altar. The high altar has three panels which are painted gold and black. The central panel portrays the Adoration of the Magi, the panel on the left is of the Annunciation and that on the right is of the Presentation in the Temple. At each end and also between these panels are four standing angels who could represent the four great archangels – Michael, Gabriel, Raphael and Uriel. They are holding shields, on which are portrayed from left to right: a chalice and Host, the Agnus Dei with the Banner of the Cross, a pelican in its piety and a cross with an entwined serpent.

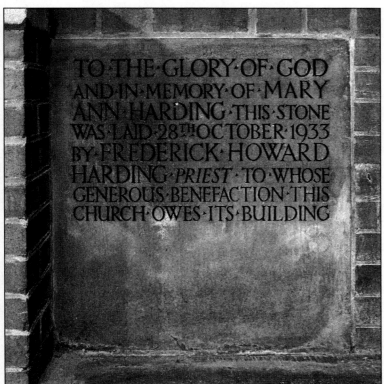

Foundation stone 1933.

Apse facing Great West Road.

The sedilia has three Shearman style wooden seats placed in it and is very similar to St. Barnabas, Cranbourne Gardens. From the chancel there are two large Gothic arches to each of the side chapels. To the south of the chancel only one of the arches allows access.

Through a narrow Gothic shaped entrance to the north of the chancel is the Transfiguration Chapel, furnished in memory of Father Harding in 1957-8. To the south through a similar entrance is the lady chapel (previously known as the Blessed Sacrament chapel). The statue of Our Lady is supported by a small Martin Travers canopy with aureole around the figure. In the lady chapel there is a bronze art-deco aumbry set in a panel of green marble. On the door of the aumbry are three vine leaves but the escutcheon to the lock has been lost. It is likely that it would have been in the form of a bunch of grapes with purple stones (as at St. Barnabas, Temple Fortune). Below the aumbry is a smaller chrism safe also set in green marble. In the first bay of the south aisle is the Walsingham Chapel.

The apse is lit by tall lancets in an Early English style with reticulated tracery; the later motifs are continued in the windows of the nave. There are pairs of clerestory lancet windows in the false transepts and also above the third and fourth bays. In the north and south chapels are some smaller reticulated two-light windows.

The glory of the church is, in the writer's opinion, the magnificent west rose window, which is the culmination of all Shearman's work. The clear glass shows the intricate leading which is a joy to study. There is no stained glass in this window or in the church.

The north-sited pulpit is set on a brick plinth and has a tester which looks like the work of Shearman. However, the stations of the cross are not in the same mould as the other Shearman churches.

There is a gilded 15 foot Rood Cross with a 7ft 6ins. figure of Christ made of lime wood hanging at the junction of the nave and chancel arch. It is the work of Miss Freda Skinner of Putney and was added to the church on Easter Sunday 1959. It was dedicated by Father Pollock.

As with his other churches, Shearman designed St. Francis for Anglo-Catholic worship, a tradition which has been maintained here for many years.

This powerful composition shows the richness of Gothic design in

Apse facing Great West Road.

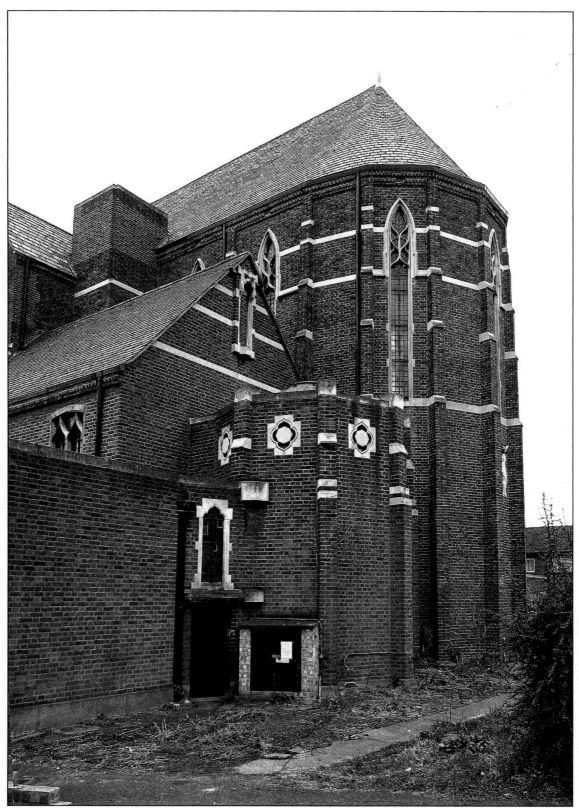

Apse and south chapel.

the 1930s, of which Shearman was one of the greatest exponents. He managed to create monumental spaces out of simple materials.

Priests-in-Charge of St. Francis of Assisi:-

1933	Frederick Howard Harding
1935	O.M. Clarke (Appointed Assistant Priest)
1936	J.G. Murray
1938	H. Nicholson
1946	Bernard H. Kemp
1950	Norman S. Pollock
1966	John Herbert Brewer
1978	Geoffrey Raymond Smith
1983	Driss R. Knickerbocker (Interregnum held by visiting American priest)
1984	David John Houghton
1991	Kevin David Moule
1995	Richard James Southerden Burn
2000	Lawrence Paul Smith

West window.

Vicarage adjoining south side of church.

False south transept.

Close-up of circular window in false south transept.

East end.

North arcade.

South arcade.

High Altar.

Sanctuary arches.

North chapel.

South chapel.

Martin Travers canopy, south chapel.

West end gallery.

South passage aisle shrine.

North passage aisle.

Nave windows.

151

Nave window.

Apse window.

Sedilia and piscina.

Arches in south chapel.

Pulpit.

Arches in south chapel.

Aumbry and chrism safe.

Font.

Pulpit.

OTHER ECCLESIASTICAL WORK
HOLY TRINITY, LAMOS DE ZAMORA

Shearman's first ecclesiastical commission was the design of the chancel, vestry and organ chamber for Trinity Church (after 1892 known as the Anglican Church of the Holy Trinity) at Lamos de Zamora, Argentina. The work done by Shearman was in brick and foreshadowed his later work on the churches in London. It contrasts with the original building, which had a cement cladding. The chancel was constructed as an apse with seven small single-light lancet windows and external buttresses between each window. Internally most of the brickwork is visible, with a piscina on the south side and a credence shelf of the same design built into the brickwork on the north side of the apse. There is a three panel stone reredos which illustrates the deposition of Christ's body in the tomb, the ascension and the women at the grave. The floor has typical Victorian tiles. Shearman arranged for stained glass to be added to the apse windows at a cost of £19 per window. The glass, of exceptionally good quality, depicts Revelations 7.12, was designed by Charles Hardgrave of James Powell & Sons but was not installed until 1896-8, after both Shearman and Father Pinchard had left Argentina. The vestry is on the north side of the chancel and has three lancet windows and an exterior doorway. The organ chamber is to the south of the chancel and also has its own exterior doorway. The organ can be seen through a broad Gothic arch. It would also appear that Shearman opened the south wall of the nave in order to provide a lady chapel as the brickwork is very reminiscent of the arcades in his London churches.

Holy Trinity, Lamas de Zamora, Buenos Aires.

Holy Trinity, Lamas de Zamora, Buenos Aires – apse.

Holy Trinity, Lamas de Zamora, Buenos Aires – chancel view from N.

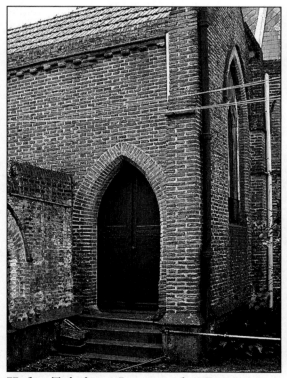

Holy Trinity, Lamas de Zamora, – door into organ chamber.

Holy Trinity, Lamas de Zamora, – door into lady chapel.

Holy Trinity, Lamas de Zamora, – west and north elevations.

Holy Trinity, Lamas de Zamora, Buenos Aires – vestry.

Holy Trinity, Lamas de Zamora, Buenos Aires – vestry.

Holy Trinity, Lamas de Zamora, Buenos Aires – nave.

Holy Trinity, Lamas de Zamora, Buenos Aires – nave.

Holy Trinity, Lamas de Zamora, Buenos Aires – sanctuary.

**Holy Trinity, Lamas
de Zamora, Buenos
Aires – reredos.**

**Holy Trinity, Lamas
de Zamora, Buenos
Aires – piscina.**

Holy Trinity, Lamas de Zamora, Buenos Aires – organ.

Holy Trinity, Lamas de Zamora, Buenos Aires – sanctuary roof.

ST. MARK'S, LEICESTER

Shearman's first church building commission in this country appears to have been to plan and construct the western extension of St. Mark's, Belgrave Gate, Leicester, which had been an incomplete work of Ewan Christian.

Christian had designed this Evangelical church in 1870-3 with an emphasis on preaching. However, styles of worship began to change with the second incumbent and even more so by the third, Canon Donaldson, vicar from 1896 to 1918. The services had by then become ritualistic.

It was during this incumbency that Shearman was asked to extend the church. Christian's original design was restricted by the limitations of the site, but when land became available, Shearman was asked to extend the church. The 33-foot extension was intended to increase the accommodation of the church by 200. The cost of approximately £5,000 was largely paid by Mrs. Sophia Perry Herrick, widow of William P. Herrick who originally paid for Christian's church in its entirety. A modest grant of £50 was also received from the Incorporated Church Building Society which was raised by £25 due to increased costs.

The existing church already had an apse, a feature that Shearman was to adopt elsewhere, nave and south clock tower with spire. The west end had a south-west porch leading into a triangular vestibule. Shearman was able to add another bay to this three bay church. He retained the south side of Christian's vestibule to

St Mark, Leicester – organ loft.

161

St Mark, Leicester.

light the extension and he repositioned the porch to face south.

Christian's west wall, including its five-light lancet window, was moved and rebuilt. In Shearman's extension, together with extra seating, he also incorporated an organ loft and a north-west entrance. The font was repositioned centrally below the gallery. In Shearman's plan the churchwardens' vestry became the vicar's vestry, thus allowing processions. Plans for this project were submitted in 1903 from 53 Berners Street and work was completed in 1904.

Brian Buchanan and Graham Hulme, in their book on St. Mark's Church, state that "Shearman's one-bay western extension imitates Christian's work, but is inferior to it." In appearance there are minor differences in the decorative detail and a significant change in the grouping of the clerestory windows in relation to the arcade which lacks the spirit of the original. The mouldings are not as fine and the decoration on the abaci less rich.

It would appear from the following letter from Shearman to the ICBS that there had been some problems with the project:

Confidential

> 53 Berners Street,
> London W
> Exning, Newmarket
> 16 Nov 1904
> Dear Sir,
>
> St. Mark's Leicester.
>
> I have no wish to be as petty to these people as they are to me.
> The work was practically done when I withdrew.
> The vicar very foolishly forced a quarrel on me – for a very paltry reason in my judgement.
> He may have asked some other architect to replace me.
> He probably thought himself more than equal to the task alone.
> [I think that is what he wanted + all the kudos.]
> If another man has not been called in, I don't think I mind giving you a plan of the church as I left it & I can find out from the builders if any minor changes were made.
> Kindly let me have the plan you have received – I shall be better able to gauge what is the right thing to do. I will return it of course.
> I certainly don't grudge your Society any courtesy.
>
> Yrs. ffly.
>
> Ernest C. Shearman

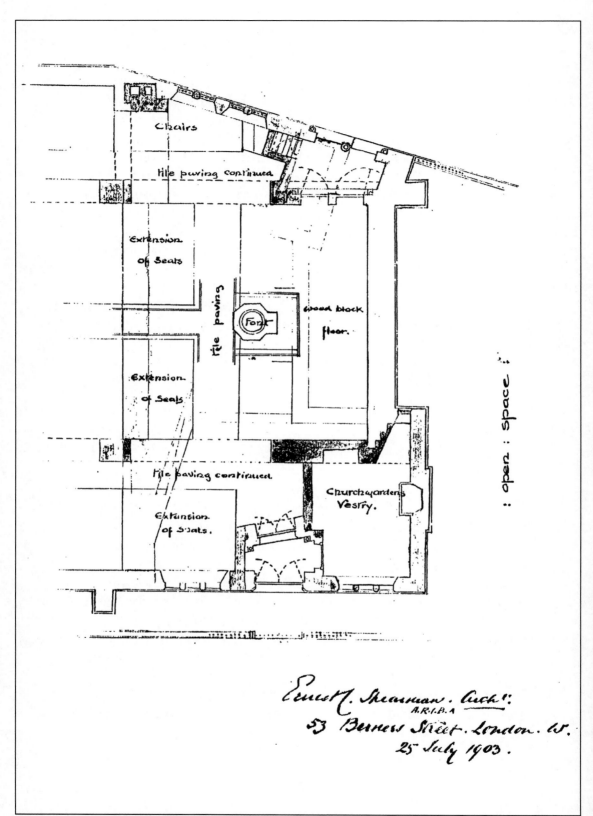

St Mark, Leicester – architect's ground plan.

ST JUDE, HILL STREET, BIRMINGHAM

The city centre church of St. Jude, Hill Street, Birmingham was built by C.W. Orford in 1850-1 and was demolished in 1965-6.

Following his return from Argentina, Father Arnold Pinchard became parish priest of this church and while there became well known as a leader of the Anglo-Catholic cause and as a Christian Socialist. He was instrumental during his time in Birmingham in founding an order for women, the Society of the Precious Blood, which in due course became enclosed and is now at Burnham Abbey, near Slough. After the First World War Father Pinchard became Secretary of the Church Union. His younger brother, the Revd. John Lester Biddulph Pinchard, was a well known priest in London. He was vicar of St. John the Baptist, Holland Road for many years and a Guardian of the Shrine of our Lady of Walsingham. It appears to have been as a result of that friendship and connection that Shearman was asked to design the lady chapel at the church. The date is uncertain but was after 1910.

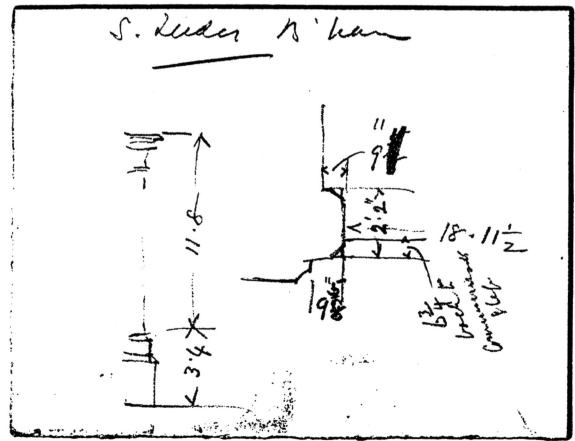

St Jude, Birmingham – sketch.

On 16th February 1901 Shearman wrote from Winchester to his daughter Elsie (then 14) describing vividly the requiem for Queen Victoria which had been held at St. Jude. The letter is worth quoting in full for the description it gives and it shows also the architect's musical interests:

"My dear Elsie,

It is my turn to write to you, I am told; also that you wanted to know how the Queen's Requiem went off at S. Jude's, Birmingham.

The "Daily Post", the leading morning paper of that City seemed to think it was something to write about, spoke well of us.

First of all, the church was packed, end to end, and nearly 300 people turned away: a great number of men in the congregation: one row near to us was all men.

All were in the deepest black: we being up the church from the west end, you know, and to sing over that sea of black was very solemn, especially when you are the only person singing (as I was, once or twice) and the black sea quiet and motionless.

Again, after the Sanctus, when the sea knelt down and left the soprano and me standing up alone (for the Benedictus duet) it had a most extraordinary effect – like the sudden dropping of the water level – and stirred us two up to do our best. We were told it was very fine, but we could not tell, ourselves; all we realized was that we had our voices and were well together, and that the piano and organ were just as we liked them to be. I wish you had been there.

Lester Pinchard told me afterwards he was listening so intently that he nearly stopped playing once.

The whole service went much better than on All Souls, and Lester's Dead March at the end was the best played of any I heard at that period of mourning.

He wrote a special Antiphon for me to the words in the Special Service. "I heard a voice from Heaven, saying unto me, write – thus saith the Spirit – Blessed are the dead which die in the Lord, for they rest from their labours, and their works do follow them. They shall stand before God's Throne and serve him day and night: and the Lamb shall lead them forth by fountains of living waters, and God shall wipe away all tears from their eyes." One of the sweetest things to sing I was ever asked to do, the last verse being lovely.

We had it again on the Sunday in the Special Memorial

Service. He wrote it only the Wednesday before!

We had the <u>drums</u> for the Dead March: our friend xx then refused an offer of £3.3. to play elsewhere – saying if we would pay his expenses (15/-) he would sooner come to us – as our Service <u>meant</u> something!

Mr. Pinchard said afterwards, it was a Service, the like of which has not been given in Birmingham since the Reformation. I wish you could have been there: you would have heard how a girl can sing, when she has a good voice and isn't afraid of hearing herself in a big church.

The hymns were 1st "Day of Wrath, Day of Mourning" which we left almost entirely to the congregation.

2nd "Now the Labourer's Task is O'er," which we were told we sang as if <u>we loved it:</u> quite true we do. Last "On the Resurrection Morning" – where (we heard afterwards) we went off at a hard gallop, leaving the congregation aghast. They picked us up in the slower parts, but soon lost us again. Peace be with them, our very reverent and loyal black sea. The solemnity and reverence of the whole service, no one could forget who was there.

Up in the square, above the Church, stands the new statue of the Queen – banked up with flowers, as never statue of any one was before – and here came thousands of people, partly bringing flowers to add to the heap, the rest looking on – or passing slowly round the barriers put up to protect the flowers.

At midnight, there were still some 200 people, wandering round, trying to read the inscriptions on the crosses and wreaths.

I think it was the most genuine tribute of homage I have ever seen, or heard of small poor children spent their pennies on violets, and threw them on to the pile. They had never seen the Queen and it was all they could do.

You will be glad to know that it is a fine statue, in white marble, a noble queenly figure in a noble position – Queen and Empress, every inch.

On the Monday we have the Christening of Arnold Patrick Biddulph who behaved himself in a most exemplary manner.

The same evening I returned.

Now I have told you everything of what we did: Betty and Joan are very flourishing.

Our Joan is in great form also – Charlie has the chickenpox, along with some others, but very mildly.

Bye, bye dearie.

Your loving Daddie."

Christ Church, Wimbledon – sanctuary.

CHRIST CHURCH, COPSE HILL, WIMBLEDON

In 1907 extensive alterations to the sanctuary were planned for this church. The reasons for the undertaking are not recorded but it is thought that it might have been for the fiftieth anniversary of the dedication of the church which was in 1909. However this was not to be and the work was not completed until 1912-1913.

It is reported in the *History of Christ Church* by Robert Willis, published in 1972, that E. C. Shearman was responsible for the whole design.

It is reported that the east window was cut away below the window and the altar set back in the recess that was formed. A new reredos of stone and marble and a white and gold canopy were erected. The communion rail and step were brought forward two feet into the sanctuary, the floor of which was inlaid with carrara marble and panels of onyx originally quarried in Mexico. The arcading removed from the east wall was re-erected as a sedilia in the south wall of the sanctuary. Then the sanctuary and chancel were redecorated and the rest of the church cleaned and distempered. Finally a new heating system was installed.

After the bombing of St Matthew's Church in June 1944 the congregation used Christ Church for their Sunday Sung Eucharist for a number of years.

Christ Church, Wimbledon.

Christ Church, Wimbledon – piscina & sedilia.

Christ Church, Wimbledon – reredos.

Christ Church, Wimbledon – sanctuary roof.

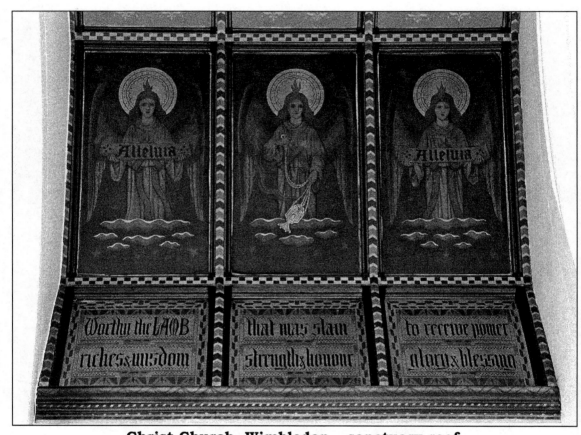

Christ Church, Wimbledon – sanctuary roof.

ST. MARY,
ST. BRIAVELS, GLOUCESTERSHIRE

Shearman designed the east window of the chancel at St. Mary in the village of St. Briavels, Gloucestershire, which was his wife's home parish. The window was made by Whitefriars. It appears to be the only occasion when he designed glass for a church he was not building himself.

A central upper six lobed window depicts Christ the King, seated, holding an orb in his left hand and giving a blessing with the right. On either side of the figure of Christ are two censing angels. On either side are smaller quatrefoil windows with the symbols alpha and omega.

The three main lights are of Mary the Virgin holding the infant Christ, flanked to the left by St. John the Baptist and to the right by St. John the Evangelist. Beneath each figure are scenes from the Nativity: Mary, Joseph and the Babe in the centre, with a similar sized panel on the left depicting the shepherds and to the right a panel of the three Magi.

The overall colours are of reds, blues and gold with a mosaic appearance.

The text in the window reads "Behold the Lamb of God – Unto us a Child is Born – The Word was made Flesh".
As with Shearman's architectural work, so with his stained glass there are subtle symbolic references. In the Nativity we see a background of vines and the base of the crib forms a simple wooden cross anticipating the passion and crucifixion. More obviously he has included an alpha and omega on either side of the upper central window of Christ the King. Surrounding all the windows are depicted the kingly crown interspersed by roses which would contrast it with the crown of thorns.

The inscription on the window reads: "To the Glory of God and in memory of William Taprell Allen MA, vicar of this Parish 1867 – 1899 and his wife Mary Mann. Given by their daughter Beatrice Julia Taylor".

The Revd. W.T. Allen had of course married Shearman and his wife in 1885. The date of the window is not certain, but it must be after 1908, which is the year in which the former vicar died. The editors of *Buildings of England* say it was as late as 1929-30.

St Mary, St Briavels,
Gloucestershire – east window
showing the Madonna & child.

St Mary, St Briavels,
Gloucestershire – east window
showing St John the Evangelist.

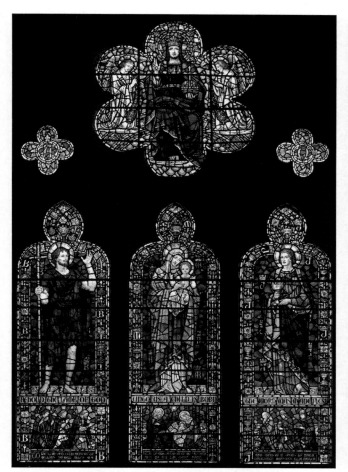

St Mary, St Briavels, Gloucestershire – east window complete.

St Mary, St Briavels, Gloucestershire – east window showing St John the Baptist.

St Mary, St Briavels, Gloucestershire – east window showing the shepherd.

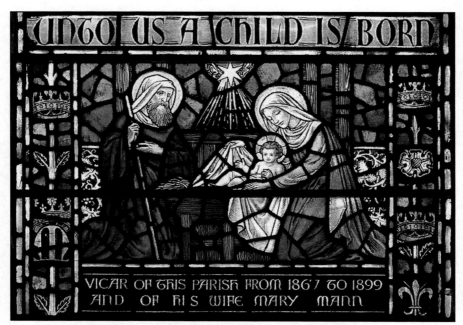

**St Mary, St Briavels, Gloucestershire –
east window showing the Nativity.**

**St Mary, St Briavels, Gloucestershire –
east window showing the Magi.**

NON ECCLESIASTICAL WORK
WATERCOLOURS AND SKETCHES

During my research into the life and times of Ernest Shearman and thanks to Jeane Duffey, Shearman's granddaughter, I have had access to copies of various small sketches and watercolours which have illustrated his abilities as an artist. These have shown a skill and a sense of humour which would not have been apparent from his architectural work. Two particular sketches illustrate this, the one called the "The Quarrel" where a boy and girl sit back to back; and also the sketch called "Bed with Insects" which probably portrays a nightmare.

Even Shearman's simple sketches of the dog, the man and

We have had enough of this:
All folk must sometime quarrel —
That there can be too much of bliss
Would seem to be the moral!

The Quarrell.

priests show how his doodles had merit. There are also a small number of more complete works which no doubt show locations visited by Shearman.

I have also included one sketch of an altar frontal showing the detail with which Shearman undertook his church work. It is not known if this work was ever completed.

Jeane Duffey advised me that she has many other items of Shearman's work but unfortunately was not able to access them and make them available to me. However, I have been able to include a few pictures by other members of Shearman's family.

Sketch of man.

Sketch of dog.

Bed of Insects (The Nightmare).

Sketch of two priests – Padre Wallis & Fr. Arnold Pinchard.

Sketch of two priests – enhanced to show greater detail in figures.

Drawing of Newmarket House by ECS.

Drawing of House by ECS or CEGS.

Pen and ink drawing of Queen of the Fens.

Sketch of house.

Snailwell . Rectory

March 2nd
19 07

Watercolour Snailwell Rectory.

May 28. 188_

St. Mary's Church
&
Town Hall
Wallingford

Marian Shearman's Sketch of St Mary, Wallingford, Berkshire.

186

Drawing of Saint by EMS for ECS.

Sketch of cow.

Sketch of tree.

Watercolour Ely from Stechworth, Cambridgeshire.

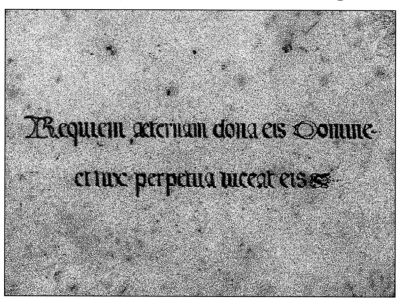

Requiem Card.

189

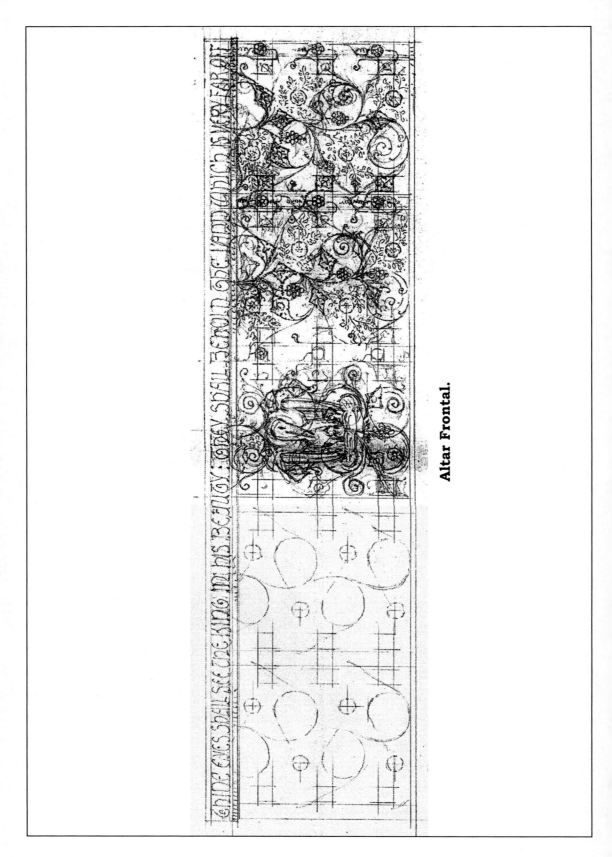

Altar Frontal.

Shearman's letter to his daughter Elsie Margaret regarding his attendance at a Requiem Mass for Queen Victoria held at St Jude's Church, Birmingham

Byrnebuscot. Winchester. 16. 2. 1901

My dear Elsie

It is my turn to write to you, I am told; also that you wanted to know how the Queen's Requiem went off at S. Jude. Birmingham.

The "Daily Post", the leading morning paper of that City seemed to think it was something to write about, spoke well of us.

First of all, the Church was packed, end to end, and nearly 300 people turned away: a great number of men in the congregation: one row near us was all men.

All were in the deepest black: we sing up the Church from the West End, you know. To sing over that sea of black was very solemn, especially when you are the only person singing (as I was, once or twice) and the black sea quiet & motionless.

Again, after the Sanctus, when the sea knelt down & left the Sopranos & me standing up alone (for the Benedictus duet) it had a most extraordinary effect, like the sudden dropping of the water level — and stirred us two up to do our best. We were told it was very fine, but we could not tell, ourselves; all we realized was that we had our voices & were well together, and that the pianos & organ were just as we liked them & c. I wish you had been there.

Lester Pinchard told me afterwards he was listening so intently that he nearly stopped playing once.

The whole Service went much better than on All Souls.

and Lester's Dead March at the end was the best played of any I heard at that period of mourning.

He wrote a special Antiphon for me to the words in the Special Service. "I heard a voice from Heaven, saying "unto me, write — Thus saith the Spirit — Blessed are the dead which "die in the Lord, for they rest from their labours, and their works "do follow them. They shall stand before God's Throne & serve him "day & night: and the Lamb shall lead them forth by fountains "of living waters, and God shall wipe away all tears from "their eyes." One of the sweetest things to sing I was ever asked to do. the last verse being lovely.

We had it again on the Sunday in the Special Memorial Service — He wrote it only the Wednesday before!

We had the dreams for the dead March: our friend of the refused an offer of £3. 3. to play elsewhere — saying if we would pay his expenses (15/-) he would rather come to us — as our Service meant something!

Mr. Pinchard said afterwards, it was a Service, the like of which has not be given in Birmingham since the Reformation. I wish you could have been there: you would have heard how a girl can sing, when she has a good voice & isn't afraid of hearing herself, in a big Church.

The hymns were 1st "Day of wrath, day of mourning" — which we left almost entirely to the Congregation.
2nd "Now the labourer's task is o'er", which we were told we sang as if we loved it: quite true, we do. Last, "On the Resurrection morning" — where (we heard afterwards) we went off at a hand gallop, leaving the Congregation aghast. They kicked us up in the slower parts, but soon lost us again. Peace be with them, our very reverent & loyal black sea. The solemnity & reverence of the whole Service, no one could forget who was there.

Up in the Square, above the Church, stands the New Statue of The Queen. Banked up with flowers, as never statue of any one was before. And here came thousands of people, partly bringing flowers to add to the heap, the rest looking on — or passing slowly round the barrier put up to protect the flowers.

At midnight, there were still some 200 people, wandering round, trying to read the inscriptions on the crosses & wreaths.

I think it was the most genuine tribute of homage I have ever seen, or heard of. Small poor children spent their pennies on violets, & threw them on to the pile — They had never seen The Queen & it was all they could do.

You will be glad to know it is a fine statue, in white marble, a noble queenly figure in a noble position — Queen & Empress, every inch.

On the Tuesday we had the Christening of Arnold Patrick Biddulph. Who behaved himself in a most exemplary manner.

The same evening I returned.

Now I have told you everything of what we did. Betty & Joan are very flourishing.

Our Joan is in great form also — Charlie has the Chicken pox, along with some others, but very mildly.

Bye, bye, dearie. Your loving Daddie.